IN A WORLD GONE MAD

8-28-2003

For Emily,
    Never to forget!
    Never to forgive!
Best wishes,
        Norman Salsitz.

IN A WORLD GONE MAD

*A Heroic Story of Love,
Faith, and Survival*

AMY HILL HEARTH

and Norman & Amalie Petranker Salsitz

ABINGDON PRESS / NASHVILLE

IN A WORLD GONE MAD
A HEROIC STORY OF LOVE, FAITH, AND SURVIVAL

This book is printed on acid-free paper.

Library of Congress Cataloging-in-Publication Data

Hearth, Amy Hill, 1958-
  In a world gone mad : a heroic story of love, faith, and survival / Amy Hill Hearth and Norman & Amalie Petranker Salsitz.
     p. cm.
  ISBN 0-687-09610-3
  1. Salsitz, Amalie Petranker, 1922- 2. Salsitz, Norman, 1920- 3. Jews—Poland—Biography. 4. Holocaust, Jewish (1939–1945) 5. Holocaust survivors—United States—Biography. 6. Jews—United States—Biography. 7. Poland—Biography. 8. United States—Biography. I. Title.

DS135.P63 A142 2001
940.53'18'0922—dc21

                                                            2001027950

01 02 03 04 05 06 07 08 09 10—10 9 8 7 6 5 4 3 2 1

MANUFACTURED IN THE UNITED STATES OF AMERICA

*To my parents, Dorothy Scheer Hill and Lee H. Hill Jr.,
who taught me the meaning of compassion*
— A.H.H.

*To our daughter, Esther S. Dezube, her husband Dr. Bruce
Dezube, and their sons, Dustin, Aaron, and Michael*
—N.S. and A.P.S.

Preface

The idea of writing this book originates from advice given to me by two very wise women, the famed centenarian Delany sisters, on a warm summer afternoon in 1995.

As coauthors of *Having Our Say: The Delany Sisters' First 100 Years*, we had watched with surprise as our project, which started with a *New York Times* article I wrote about them in 1991, became a critically acclaimed best-seller. The book was then adapted to the Broadway stage, and plans were already well under way for a film adaptation.

Life was good.

The question I had for my two wise friends was: What next? What I meant was, What will I do after you are gone?

They were both over one hundred, but I was only in my thirties. I wanted to write more books. But about what? I had so many interests—too many. There were so many directions I could follow.

"Well," said the wise centenarians, speaking at the same time, which they did frequently, "you are young, and you can have a brilliant career ahead of you. Or you can waste your time."

"Waste my time?" Of course, I didn't want to do that.

"You must choose something that is worthy of your time and God-given talent," declared the feisty younger sister,

Bessie. The elder sister—we called her Sweet Sadie—nodded her head in agreement. "Child," she said encouragingly, "I am sure you will choose well."

"Well, how will I know it will be the right project?"

"You will just know," they said in unison.

I must have looked a little dissatisfied with the answer. I needed something a little more specific.

Bessie, reading my mind, hesitated a moment and then slowly and emphatically said, *Do the hardest thing you can think of.*

What she meant was that only something difficult would be worthwhile. She was saying that she wanted me to challenge myself, but that the result would be worth it.

As the reader will find out, "the hardest thing" for me meant writing about the Second World War and, specifically, about a Jewish person or persons who had survived the persecution of the Germans. As a Christian whose mother is German-American, I had always avoided the entire subject.

I had my topic but not the next step. Then one day, in a local newspaper, I spotted an article about a Jewish couple who lived about an hour away and who were raising funds for "Righteous Gentiles"—Christians who had saved or tried to save a Jew during the war. The article mentioned that the man and woman, who met near the end of the war, had avoided the Nazi death camps by masquerading as Christians, a nearly impossible task—that much I knew—in Nazi-occupied Poland.

They were somewhat legendary, it turns out, in the tightly knit world of Jewish Holocaust survivors, but not known elsewhere. I wondered whether there was a way to tell their unusual story to a broad and diverse audience and at the same time chronicle my thoughts and feelings as I faced, in Bessie's words, "the hardest thing" I could think of.

The couple agreed to let me into their lives, as did their daughter, her extended family, and other friends and relatives. I learned about life and death, about outwitting the Gestapo, and about a world gone mad. But I also learned about a couple who found love in the midst of it all, who rebuilt their lives together and faced the future with hope, courage, ferocity, and even, at times, humor.

Happily, another dimension of the book arose: the chronicling of earned respect and, eventually, friendship between this Christian writer and an elderly pair of Jewish Holocaust survivors.

That is how this book came about. It is born of good intentions and a promise kept.

Contents

PART TWO

THE JOURNEY BEGINS

The cemetery down the road from the little Lutheran church had not changed in more than twenty years, not since that day of wilted flowers and glowering gravediggers, which is all I remember clearly now. The day of my grandmother's burial in 1975 was unbearably hot. She was put in the ground beside my grandfather, who had died a year earlier.

I had been there since then, of course. Once I saw a double rainbow, like angels holding hands across the valley. Another time I was bitten by a spider. I vowed never to return, but I did.

It was the first time I had returned with my mother. It was early fall 1998. The cemetery sits high on a hill overlooking a farm much like the one my grandparents owned just a mile down the road. The apples on the trees in the orchard bobbed heavily in the slightest breeze.

My mother spoke of practical things. The evergreens she planted beside the grave died. Didn't my brother try to prune them once, but they had grown too large? Who finally removed them? Was it the farmer, the one whose job it was to keep the cemetery mowed and groomed? Oh, well. We must plant something next time we come. It's too hot today anyway. Anything we plant will wither and die....

I was not really listening. My mind shifted back to a phone

conversation two weeks earlier. As a writer, I hoped to interview an elderly Jewish couple, a husband and wife named Norman and Amalie Petranker Salsitz who survived the Holocaust in Poland by masquerading as Christians and working for the underground.

I had no idea then that I was about to embark on a book project that would enter my subconscious, causing me to dream fitfully at night of black-booted thugs in German Army uniforms, of ghettos, false identification papers, harrowing escapes and heroic deeds. Little did I know that this project would take me as far away as Jerusalem.

Early in our first phone conversation the man abruptly asked me, "May I ask what nationality you are?"

"I'm an American," I said quickly, perhaps too quickly.

"Well, I'm an American, too, now," he replied, laughing. "I mean, what nationality are your parents? What is your background?"

"My father is English, Scottish, Danish, and German," I said, trying to skip quickly over the last word. "His family has been here for a long time; he's a twelfth-generation American."

"Oh! Like the *Mayflower*," he said.

"Well, almost. Just after that."

"And your mother?"

I felt my face flush. "My mother is a first-generation American, born in Chicago," I heard myself saying. "Her parents were German and came to the U.S. in 1920 from an ethnic German colony called Sekic in Yugoslavia."

"Oh," he said. I wondered whether he was going to hang up the phone, but after a pause he added, "Well, you're certainly not Jewish."

"No, I'm not. I'm Christian. Protestant. Methodist, as a matter of fact."

16

My professional demeanor was unraveling like the frayed edges of the old knitted slippers that my German grandmother made for me as a teenager and that I still sometimes wear. So that was what it all came down to. Three newspaper jobs and three books on my résumé, but at that precise moment they meant nothing. All that mattered was something completely out of my control, the circumstances of my being.

On the other hand, I could understand his point of view. What Holocaust survivor was going to let me into his house? Why should he?

I remember the first time I heard about the Holocaust in school, in fifth or sixth grade. I was relieved that my grandparents had left Europe in 1920, before the atrocities began. But what if they had stayed in Europe? Would they have participated in the greatest crime of all time? Would my mother? Would I?

These are the questions that sometimes haunt those of us with German ancestry, even Americans such as myself. Indeed, my father was a U.S. Army enlisted man who served in China from 1943 to 1946. My father, it was clear to me as a child, had been one of the good guys. But if that was so, then how to explain my mother's parents, who spoke German and lived in a place called Germantown, New York, who smiled and fed me and scolded me and loved me, and yet—I was to learn in school one day—were cut from the same cloth as the worst human beings who ever lived?

I clutched the phone while the Holocaust survivor mulled it over. Finally, he spoke again. "Well, I find it very interesting that you are interested," he said. The tone of his voice had changed, and at first I didn't know how to interpret it. He was more subdued and contemplative, as if he was speaking to himself. Then he added, "If you didn't have the right feelings, you wouldn't have contacted me in the first place. Why don't you come here and meet me and my wife?"

My mother was speaking aloud again, and my attention returned to her as we stood before the graves of her parents at the cemetery on the hill in Germantown. "They lived a hard life," she was saying, and I nodded in agreement. She sighed. I know all the stories: the notorious swine flu epidemic, which stole both of their mothers (my great-grandmothers); World War I, in which my grandfather, a teenager, was forced to serve; the bold choice to immigrate to America in 1920 as a young couple; the factory work that ruined the eyes and the spirit; the depression years in Chicago and New York, living on rotted fruit and, from time to time, being quarantined for disease; World War II, which destroyed their hometown in Europe and any dreams of returning; the struggle to become Americans and to make ends meet on a small fruit farm where they lived basically hand-to-mouth in the Hudson Valley of New York State.

I remember my grandparents as very human, arguing frequently about things I did not understand. My grandmother, whose name was the anglophilic-sounding Barbara, was emotional and passionate. My grandfather, John Scheer, would turn down his hearing aid to literally tune her out. But while they were sometimes savage with each other, they were tender with me. Grandpa was somewhat aloof but possessed a warm smile. Grandma was known for hugs that would knock the stuffing out of you. She taught me to say bedtime prayers in German, and once, when she thought I was already asleep, she said "I love you more than I love myself."

My grandparents are on my mind all the following week as I get ready to meet Mr. and Mrs. Salsitz. I had always thought of my grandparents, as my mother had said at the cemetery, as having lived a hard life. Compared to some people, yes. But not at all compared to Norman and Amalie Salsitz; that much would surely be true.

The day finally arrives, and I leave so early for the forty-five-minute drive from my house, at the New Jersey shore, to theirs, in Springfield, New Jersey, that I end up sitting in my car on a side street, staring at my watch anxiously.

All around me are the comforting rhythms of typical American suburban life. It is a long way from Poland during World War II. People walk their dogs as if they don't have a care in the world, and perhaps they don't.

It is a Thursday morning, and garbage cans are arranged in perfect choreography from one driveway to the next as far as the eye can see. The neighborhood is pleasant and well kept, the lawns neatly mowed and the houses freshly painted. I notice that in several yards, a statue of Mary is displayed.

The cream-colored house on the corner is not noticeably different from any other, but at exactly eleven o'clock, as I pull into the driveway, I notice a woman sitting on the landing at the top of the steps leading to the house. She is mostly hidden behind shrubbery. Her watchfulness makes me self-conscious, and I am relieved when she welcomes me with a brilliant smile and, taking my hand, invites me to join her on the backyard patio.

"It is too beautiful to sit indoors today, don't you think?" she says, leading me through the house and out the back. "I love to sit outside. One can find peace in nature."

We settle into the patio furniture, and I take out my notebook and tape recorder. Sitting here in her backyard under a yellow-and-white umbrella to protect her complexion from the summer sun, she appears years younger. She is still stunning at seventy-six years old. Quickly, however, I learn that she is not only beautiful, but blunt and to the point.

"Why are you here, my dear; I mean really?"

"I'm a journalist," I answer, thinking that should suffice. She looks at me as if to say, "And?"

"And, well, the Jewish Holocaust was one of the most important events of the twentieth century—of the history of the world. I want to understand it. I want to learn what you know."

She stares at me intently, a tight smile on her lips, and for a moment I am sorry that I have come.

"I guess I am asking a lot of you," I say apologetically. I wait for a moment as a plane passes overhead. "I don't so much want you to repeat the facts of what happened," I say simply. "I want to understand how you feel. I want to know what it is like to lose family and friends, to live through a war posing as someone else, to fall in love, of all things. I want to know about your life after the war. I want to know why you survived and how you have managed to live a normal life."

She says nothing but nods her head slightly in approval. I have surprised her. Then she surprises me.

"Are you interested as a journalist—or perhaps because your mother is German and this is a personal journey for you?"

It is an awkward and painful moment, but there's no way to duck the question. "Yes," I say, "you are right." It shouldn't be surprising, I suppose, that a woman who outwitted the Nazis, who lived by her intuition, can see right through me.

And so our conversation, or series of conversations, begins, along with a journey of understanding that would affect us all.

PART ONE

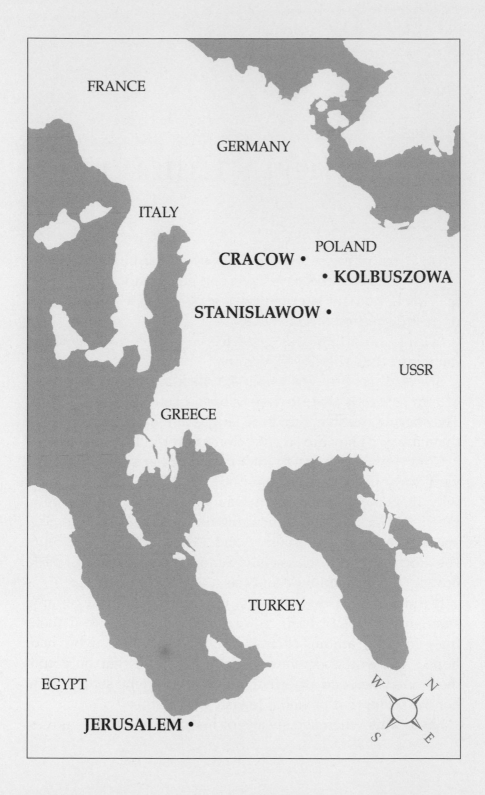

FRANCE

GERMANY

ITALY

CRACOW • POLAND

• KOLBUSZOWA

STANISLAWOW •

USSR

GREECE

TURKEY

EGYPT

JERUSALEM •

Chapter One

A Beautiful Childhood

Amalie pauses and pushes back her chair from the glass-topped patio table and goes inside. She returns a moment later with two glasses and a small pitcher of fresh-squeezed orange juice.

"Drink it, darling. It is good for you," she says, handing me mine while she sips from hers.

She also has brought peanuts, which attract the attention of two squirrels that obviously have been indulged before. They beg aggressively, and she laughs at them, trying to shoo them away. "They are so cute, don't you think?" she asks.

Conversing with her in the privacy of her sheltered backyard, forty-five minutes from midtown Manhattan, I can see why this intelligent woman was able to masquerade as a Polish or German girl, depending on the circumstances. She speaks the languages fluently, and as she herself points out, she does not look classically Semitic. Her eyes are dark brown, but she is blonde and has a fair complexion.

It did not hurt that she was unusually beautiful by any standards. It is not hard to imagine why men risked their lives for her, among them a Hungarian count, who had hoped she would convert to Catholicism so that he could then marry her, and a German businessman who shared with her the secret that he had a Jewish grandfather.

She beams when she speaks of her childhood. She moves

her hands animatedly as she speaks, an expressive habit, she says, that she acquired from an American friend, a woman of Polish Catholic descent who had married an Italian-American. "I don't think my parents would have approved at all," she says, amused at the thought.

There are few outward clues of the life Amalie has led. Only when this poised and charming woman says the word *mother* does she give herself away, for her voice trembles slightly and so does her hand as she refills my juice glass. When she speaks of the early years of her life, she leans forward slightly as if steeling herself before diving into cold water. But she plunges in and takes me with her.

She tells me that she knows she has not lived a typical life. It is not a "normal" life by most people's standards. "I had a beautiful childhood," she tells me, "a wonderful home. But by the time I was nineteen years old, I was on my own. I had to live by my wits. I can't understand how I did it, how I knew enough to be able to do it. I still don't know."

Her parents, she recalls, had a happy marriage. They met when her mother's father, Leib Genger, who was in the lumber business, had met a young man named David Petranker, who was from a town called Delatyn in the Carpathian Mountains. David Petranker was also in the lumber business and was working at a big mill in the mountains. Leib Genger liked the young man so much that he decided he wanted him for a son-in-law for his only daughter, Frieda. (He also had four sons: Max, Philip, Josef, and Herman.) He introduced them, and they fell in love.

She interrupts herself, smiling mischievously. "Grandpa was a matchmaker!"

And so it was that Frieda and David, her parents, met. They were to have three daughters: Pepka, born in 1921; Amalie, in 1922; and Celia, in 1923. Frieda, born in 1900, was

24

a young mother and was in some ways more like another sister than a mother, Amalie tells me.

"She was vivacious and easygoing, with a lovely smile and chestnut hair," Amalie says, "quite the opposite of my father in personality." Five years older than his wife, David Petranker made a more serious impression on his daughters. He was more strict, often refusing to let his daughters do things their friends were doing.

"No movies for us until we had done all our assignments from school," Amalie tells me, as if she were talking in the present.

But it was from her father, she concedes, that she got the gift of self-confidence, perhaps—she is fully aware now—one of the reasons that she survived the war. David Petranker, it seems, tended to treat his three daughters like boys, expecting them to ask questions, to be assertive, to express opinions about business and politics. (Later, a "brother" was added to the household when a young cousin of Frieda's, a young boy named Menashe, was adopted by the family.)

Amalie describes her relationship with her older sister, Pepka, as a bit of a rivalry ("We were jealous of each other at times"). Little sister, Celia, however, was "almost like my twin." Even on a date with a boy, Celia would tag along. Celia was so sweet, so kind, Amalie tells me, that she couldn't say no to her.

They lived a cultured, sophisticated life in Stanislawow, a city of about 100,000 people. Education was key. David Petranker had attended the prestigious Agricultural School of Baron Hirsch and spoke fluent German, Ukrainian, Polish, Yiddish, and Hebrew. He had also taught himself French and English. Frieda had graduated from Realschule, a prestigious school in Stanislawow with very high standards. While the family spoke mainly Polish at home, David Petranker made a point of emphasizing that his daughters knew Hebrew.

David Petranker was also a talented artist, particularly skilled at painting portraits. His artistic ability, Amalie says, probably saved him from being on the front lines in the Austrian army during World War I. He was assigned to paint proclamations and posters.

The Petranker family did not mingle much with the Christian population of the city or, for that matter, even with other Jews other than those they knew from school. Everything, at least for the girls, revolved around school.

Were Jews openly discriminated against? "Yes, they were," Amalie says. "We were pretty sheltered, we didn't feel discriminated against, but Jews were definitely treated as a different class of people."

For instance, she says, doctors could work only at the Jewish hospital. Jews had little choice but to start their own businesses in order to make a living. Amalie's father was unusual. He held a high government position. When the Polish government nationalized the lumber business in that section of Poland, David Petranker was named vice-director of the PAGED, or Polska Agencja Drzewna (Polish Lumber Agency). The director, however, was a Polish nobleman. A Jew could not be number one.

An ardent Zionist, David Petranker dreamed of the day that he could save enough money and move his family to Palestine. He sent all three of his daughters to the Hebrew kindergarten, primary school, and gymnasium, and it was very expensive. As a result, he had not saved enough money to go to Palestine before the war broke out.

In 1938, when Hitler expelled Polish Jews living in Germany, they were sent to Zbonszyn, just over the German-Polish border, and then to different towns in Poland, including Amalie's.

"It was shocking to see these poor souls," she says, drawing a deep breath. "We did many things to help them."

Suddenly, the carefree days of normal life began to recede into the past. History was happening around them, and to them. When Czechoslovakia was invaded, they sat spellbound by the radio. It was a bad sign, David Petranker said, because the Germans would want to conquer Poland, too.

He was right. On September 1, 1939, the Germans invaded Poland. After a few days the Polish army units came through Stanislawow heading east to Romania, literally on the run. The mayor then announced that the Russians would be occupying the city. And so it was, from 1939 to 1941.

One moment, Amalie tells me, is crystallized in her mind. It was after the Russian occupation was over, and the Germans were in charge. On the streets of Stanislawow, her hometown, she was assaulted by two young Polish men who hit her and tried to take her purse.

"I screamed, and do you know what? People just walked by. They didn't try to help me. This would never, never have happened in the past. The Poles were chivalrous; they were gentlemanly. They would have come to the assistance of a woman."

It was an ominous sign, she says, clutching her glass of orange juice so tightly that I worry that it might break in her hand. She looks unfocused, far away. "It is different for me than for my husband, you will see," she says confidentially, almost in a whisper.

"Why is that?"

At this moment, the screen door creaks open, cutting off our conversation abruptly. I turn to see a gray-haired man with enormous bushy eyebrows close the door behind him and step outside into the sunlight. He has the bearing of a man who has seen it all, and I wonder if perhaps he has. Although he is seventy-eight years old and walks slowly and perhaps painfully, it is not difficult to picture him escaping from German labor camps; living through brutal winters in

the woods in Poland while on the run; carrying out dangerous missions for the Polish Armia Krajowa (Home Army);
then after the liberation, becoming head of intelligence in a
unit of the Polish army while masquerading as a Catholic.

If the elegant and charming Amalie looks as though she
could be strolling along Fifth Avenue in Manhattan, her husband, Norman, looks like a warrior ready to do battle. As he
sits down, he grabs a handful of peanuts, tosses a few to the
squirrels, and gulps the rest.

"Norman, those are not for you!" Amalie scolds him.

"I am just feeding the little squirrels," he says.

"And yourself," Amalie says and laughs.

"Yes, yes, and myself," Norman says. He laughs, too. "My
wife here, she is very hard on me," he complains.

"You have interrupted us, Norman," Amalie says firmly.

"Let me tell you a story," Norman says to me, ignoring her.

"Norman! I am speaking now! It is your turn later."

Norman turns to her and makes a face.

Amalie stares back, unblinking. She says something rapidly in Polish.

"Do you know what my wife just said to me?" he says,
feigning hurt. "She just told me to shut up in Polish!"

"Oh, Norman," Amalie says with a sigh.

The squirrels, another jet plane overhead, and Norman's
arrival put an end to the private conversation with Amalie
for now. It's time to eat lunch anyway. Amalie has prepared
bagels and lox and cream cheese, fresh cucumbers, Jersey
tomatoes, rye bread, yogurt, cantaloupe, and pears. It is a hot
day for so much food. Norman chastises me for not eating
with gusto.

"She'll never finish everything on her plate," Norman says.
"Look how wasteful she is. She leaves half of everything!"

"Norman, don't be rude!" Amalie says. She pours coffee.

Pointing to my cup, Norman says to Amalie, "Give her a full cup. That way she'll drink half!"

"Norman!" Amalie says firmly. Then to me, pleasantly, "Darling, if you're a good girl and finish all your food, I will give you some Breyer's chocolate ice cream."

Norman will not be silenced. He is ready to talk. Norman is always ready to talk. "Americans do not know how lucky they are to be born here, in this great country," he declares. "If I could live my life over again, I would ask the stork not to drop me in the little Polish town of Kolbuszowa in the year 1920. No, I would ask him to drop me off in the heart of America, in New York City at the Empire State Building!"

"Norman, the Empire State Building in New York City is not the heart of America," Amalie interrupts him. "The heart of America is Kansas or Minneapolis or someplace like that near Chicago."

Norman is undeterred. "The point is, I was born at the wrong time and at the wrong place." He says this with a shrug, as if to say, "That's just the way it is."

He turns to me and speaks abruptly. "Where were you born?" he asks.

"Pittsfield, Massachusetts," I say, thinking that must sound like outer space to them.

"When?"

"April 1958." A picture flashes in my mind of a split-level, custom-built house, its cupboards, toy boxes, and bookshelves bursting with the excesses of postwar American affluence. I can almost see my college-educated parents and my three older siblings, dressed in nifty clothes, as we pile into our new Chevy station wagon to head downtown to the Methodist church on a Sunday morning. What a soft life I have lived.

Norman sighs. "Ehhhh," he says, as if reading my mind. "You are a very lucky girl indeed."

Chapter Two

OF MIND AND MEMORY

H ello, Federal Express?" Norman is almost shouting into the phone. "I want you should pick up a letter. No, not a package—a letter! A letter! No, not at a business. A residence, a private residence!"

A week has passed since my last visit. We are sitting in his home office, he swiveling in his desk chair impatiently while I sit on a small sofa with my feet elevated on a footstool. The footstool is Amalie's idea.

He is on hold while they check his account. "I guess they don't understand my accent," he says to me. Suddenly, he grins and raises one eyebrow, a sign that he is about to tell a joke or self-deprecating remark. "When I came to America in 1947," he says with a mischievous smile, "I thought I could speak English. But when I arrived in New York, I found out that this wasn't so."

Norman's first exposure to English came during the war when he studied key words that had been translated on the back page of an army manual. Amalie studied English as a foreign language for six years while a student at the gymnasium in Poland, and the result is that to this day she is more fluent. Often Norman reverts to Polish or Yiddish or Hebrew, asking Amalie for help in finding just the right word in English. It is a source of tension, in part because it is a constant reminder that she had better formal education than he, and in part because he is not the type of person who likes to ask for help.

His desk is piled haphazardly with books, file folders, letters, and scraps of paper. The letter to be picked up by Federal Express is a response to a scholar with a question about Kolbuszowa, Norman's hometown in Poland.

Norman is still fighting a war that, according to most people's timetable, ended a half-century ago. There are several major battle fronts in Norman's war, carried out through the written and the spoken word. There are the frequent skirmishes with those who would rewrite history. There is the continuous struggle to remind the world of victims who were individuals, not just numbers. And there is a never-ending effort to immortalize the lost people of prewar Kolbuszowa, a place where a way of life was virtually eliminated, except in the mind and memory of this seventy-eight-year-old man who won't, or can't, let go of it.

"Let me tell you a story," he says to me, and I realize I might as well get comfortable since this could take a while. "You know, my father, he was a storyteller. People ask a question, and I may answer by telling a story, just as my father did. It drives my wife crazy sometimes!"

So—what is the story?

"Oh, yes, I was going to tell you that I have escaped death many times. When I was a baby, I was exposed to smallpox and became very sick. In fact, they thought I was dead. My mother, she took me in her arms, and she prayed, 'Oh, God, I know I have nine children and this is the youngest and I am so lucky, but why do you have to take this, the littlest one, from me?'

"Well, my father came home, and they were all very sad. They placed me in a yeast box, which would be my coffin. The man came who was to bury me, and my father offered

31

him something to drink. The two of them, they sat there sadly.

"After a while, the man commented that he heard a noise. 'Isak, do you know you have mice in the house?' And my father said, 'Why, no, no, we have no mice. We have very fine cats. We have no mice.'

"Suddenly, they realized that the noise was coming from the yeast box. It was me, making soft, little whimpering sounds.

"Well, you can imagine how happy everyone was. And so this is how I escaped death for the first time. This is a story I heard many times growing up.

"Many times I came close to dying, but somehow I kept living. Many times it was sheer luck! Sometimes, like my wife, I look back on my life, and it seems like it must have happened to somebody else. Surely, what I have been through is too much for one person in a lifetime. I am like a cat that has—what is the saying?—nine lives. Except that I've already had a lot more than nine."

Amalie calls to me from the kitchen, inviting me to join her. When Amalie is not on the patio, she can often be found here, a room that seems off-limits to Norman except at mealtimes. The light in the kitchen is ideal for reading, she says.

Although Amalie is the perfect hostess when guests come to visit, she claims to care little for cooking and preparing meals. "There is only one thing that I cook well, and that is mushroom soup," she tells me. She is already at work on her specialty.

"Are you making that for me?" Norman shouts from his office.

"No, I am making it for our guest," she calls back, sounding annoyed. To me, she adds, "You know, Norman makes fun of my cooking. His mother and sisters were great cooks. Or so he says."

Indeed, when Amalie serves supper, Norman points to the store-bought cookies she puts out for dessert.

"See, she slaved all night making these," he says teasingly.

The tiniest flash of hurt or anger flickers across Amalie's face. She ignores him, head held high. Amalie is not a person who sulks, but her pride has indeed been tweaked.

Norman answers a phone call, and Amalie relaxes for the moment. She clearly enjoys having a guest in her kitchen. Perhaps it is because I am about the same age as her only child, Esther, who lives several hundred miles away, near Boston. Soon the conversation turns to the foibles of men, and before long we are laughing—she softly, me loudly.

Suddenly, she stops.

"What is it?" I ask, wondering if somehow I have offended.

"There is not usually laughter like that in this house unless my grandsons are visiting," she says.

It is a revealing remark, and I ask her to explain. She replies that she rarely laughs aloud and has not felt comfortable laughing, really laughing, for a long time.

How long?

She is evasive. "A long time," is all she will say. The rest of this story, I realize, will have to wait for another day.

Chapter Three

A Fateful Decision

A week goes by, and I hope that Amalie may be ready to explain her remark. We are sitting on the patio, even though it's very hot. I wait for her to speak, and at last, she does.

"Celia had a premonition," Amalie says finally, her voice sounding strained and faraway. "Our older sister, Pepka, married and moved to Palestine in 1939, and Celia cried and fainted—as if she knew she would never see Pepka again. It seemed a little strange at the time. Little did we know."

Ironically, Amalie had a chance to escape but did not take it. A Hungarian count who was serving in the Hungarian army was assigned to take over the Petranker family's apartment. The Petrankers were supposed to leave, but the count quickly became enamored of Amalie and allowed them to stay.

"He wasn't shy about his feelings toward me," Amalie tells me. "He wanted me to become a Catholic and marry him."

The count, it seems, even devised a daring plan to smuggle Amalie across the border in the trunk of his car, believing that because of his title and rank, the trunk would not be searched. Amalie's father, however, believed the plan too risky and told the count that it was not possible.

In hindsight, it would have been wise for the entire family

to have left with the Russians when that army left in 1941. Under German occupation, things rapidly worsened. David Petranker was assigned to slave labor. Beautiful, carefree Frieda spent her days waiting in line for the small amount of food the family was permitted to buy. Celia and Amalie were assigned to work at Gestapo headquarters.

The job they were given? To clean toilets. With their bare hands.

"This was so typical of the Germans," Amalie says with quiet anger. "They always made things worse by finding a way to humiliate us. They wanted to break us, not just physically but mentally, and to rob us of dignity."

It is horrible to imagine this lovely and elegant woman, with her pretty manicured nails, cleaning toilets with her bare hands. I find myself staring at her hands and then looking away. *I wouldn't do that*, I think, *but then, who knows?*

The price for defiance was high. Celia was the first in the Petrankers' close-knit family to learn how merciless the Germans could be, Amalie tells me quietly. One day, a group of Hungarian Jews was imprisoned at the courtyard of the Gestapo building, crying out for water. When she thought no one was looking, Celia took the meager lunch that Frieda had prepared for her and pushed it through the bars to the people imprisoned in the courtyard.

She was caught.

"I heard what happened and rushed to the officer in charge. Where was Celia? Where was my sister? Couldn't they just let her go?"

In her state of panic, however, Amalie had forgotten to put on her armband, the Star of David that identified her as a Jew. She had taken it off while working. By law, she had to wear it on the street.

The officer yelled at her for forgetting the armband. "It is a miracle that he didn't throw me in with the others," she says, wonderment creeping into her voice.

It fell upon Amalie to tell their parents that Celia had been taken away. Devastated, they tried every lead to find her. They did not give up hope easily.

Soon after Celia disappeared, Amalie was assigned to serve as a maid for a Gestapo officer—Daus, she says his name was—and his fiancée in the officers' living quarters. The fiancée was a nice person and offered to try to find out what had happened to Celia. The woman had seemingly good news: Celia, she was told, was working at a farm some distance away. Amalie might even be allowed to visit.

But it was a lie. All of it.

Celia, the family eventually learned, had been shot along with one hundred other girls and buried in an unmarked grave.

Neither of us says anything for a while. An airplane buzzes overhead. My mind is churning with thoughts and feelings. Celia Petranker, seventeen years old, was murdered. Killed because she had, ironically and incredibly, done the most humane thing imaginable: she shared her food with strangers who were starving. Of course, the real reason she was murdered was that she was Jewish. She had the nerve to be Jewish.

"I miss my Celia every day of my life," Amalie says softly. "What I mean is, I don't think about her every minute of the day, but she is with me constantly. You know, she could still be living today. Perhaps she would be a grandmother now like I am. But no one can know what her life would have been like. I can only remember her the way she was, just a schoolgirl, very sweet and loving."

The late-day sun has grown intense, as it does just before it peaks and begins to fade at twilight. Amalie's face is illuminated in an unsparing light, her emotions laid bare.

It is hard to look at her. I feel the shame of the journalist who has intruded. To talk to me, she must relive these sorrows. It is cruel of me to be here, to ask these questions. At this moment, I regret coming.

The tension is broken by the sound of children walking down the street. They are the voices of girls; no, they are older than that, perhaps young teenagers. It is happy noise, shrieks and mock anger and hysterical laughter. The sweet sounds are jarring.

Suddenly, the sound of the girls' voices is gone. They have vanished. Like Celia....

Amalie takes a deep breath and rises abruptly from her chair. Studying her, I learn that she finds momentary solace in changing the subject. "The mosquitoes are out; let's go back inside," she says simply.

Funny thing is, she seems worried about me. I have no doubt I am looking a little ragged. She can see that her stories have made me depressed. Yet I am almost embarrassed to admit it, for what is my sadness compared to theirs? There's no hiding your feelings in this house.

Amalie is sympathetic. "Yes, yes, it is very sad," she says soothingly. Then: "I will make you some tea." She puts on the kettle. Digging through the cupboards, she locates something, turns, and smiles triumphantly: coconut macaroons.

"Here, darling, eat these. It will make you feel better."

She confides that she has hidden the macaroons from Norman, who must keep an eye on his blood-sugar level. Since Norman apparently refuses to do so, it's up to Amalie to see that he does. It is hard to decide who finds this more irritating, Norman or Amalie.

Norman seems to have radar when it comes to sweets, and soon he is at the entryway to the kitchen, peering into the room with the alertness of a bomb-sniffing dog. "What is this I smell?" he says, accusingly, hopefully.

Amalie sighs, almost a growl. "All right, Norman, you may have one," she says, thrusting it at him.

He gobbles it and says to me mischievously, "I'll have another one if you have another one."

"Norman, you should not have any more!" Amalie scolds.

He takes one anyway and bites into it quickly, like a naughty child would, before Amalie takes the rest of the macaroons out of his reach. Amalie glares at him, then looks to me for sympathy, as if to say, "See what I have to put up with?"

She changes her tone when addressing me. "Darling, have another one," she coos. She ignores Norman. He is sulking, but resigned.

"You see, the trouble with Norman," she says to me as if Norman isn't present, "is that he was indulged as a child. He is used to getting his way."

Norman makes a remark under his breath, and suddenly, the pair begin speaking sharply in Polish.

"Do you know what my wife just said to me in Polish?" Norman complains.

It is not hard to guess.

Chapter Four

THE STORYTELLER

Norman steers his 1992 Lincoln Town Car with his left hand and looks at the hand-drawn map held in his right at the same time. He has trouble looking back and forth between the road and the map, so he moves the map, leaning it on the steering column.

"There, that's better," he says.

It is an October morning, the first cold day of the fall season. Norman is headed to Garwood, New Jersey, where he will speak at the Lincoln School, a public middle school, about his experiences during World War II. Arriving at the school at precisely 9:45, Norman is not shy. When he can't locate the principal's office immediately, he walks right into a classroom and asks for assistance.

Norman is treated like a celebrity, albeit a local one. He is welcomed by the principal, the school superintendent, a reporter from a local newspaper, and a television interviewer from a station broadcasting from nearby Secaucus, New Jersey. He is to speak to one hundred fifty students in the sixth, seventh, and eighth grades, who gather in the gymnasium.

Norman does not plan ahead for a speech. "All I want to know is the age of the kids," he says. He also says he does not mince words, believing that children know when they are being patronized. "They must understand the cruelty of it," he says.

A hush falls over the group as Norman enters and begins to speak. Considering their ages, I find the children to be surprisingly attentive.

"You look like the children of my town, pretty and smart," he tells them. "I am here to tell you about the things that I saw and did because everyone should be the watchman to be sure it doesn't happen again. Maybe if a skinhead approached you, you will know to turn away."

He tells the story of his beloved town, Kolbuszowa, and in the background we can hear younger children at recess playing outside. "Why do I do these speeches?" he asks rhetorically. "Because when I will be gone, these stories will vanish with me."

The children have been studying World War II in social studies and seem to grasp the significance of Norman's experiences and his eyewitness account. For an hour after his talk, until the teachers are forced to end the session because of time constraints, the children ask questions. They make him repeat much of what he has just said, as if they can't accept it. And they want more information. They want to know if Norman ever met Adolf Hitler (no) and did he, Norman, ever kill anyone (yes). These students, according to the superintendent of the district, are nearly all Christian, mostly Catholic, from working-class families.

After lunch, there are several other speakers, all American veterans of World War II, including the mayor of the town. Norman stays to listen to their stories. He has picked up a special fan along the way: A blue-eyed boy wearing a black-and-blue plaid flannel shirt clings to Norman. Wherever Norman goes, the boy follows, sitting next to him, standing near him. Finally, he hands Norman a piece of paper upon which he has written:

Dear Mr. Salsitz:
Thank you for coming to my school today. I learned a lot.

Norman smiles and thanks him and asks his name. The boy, suddenly shy, signs his name on the bottom of his letter. It is a German name, a non-Jewish German name. Norman laughs softly at the irony of it: the old Jew and his new little friend, the blue-eyed Aryan. Under different circumstances, at a different time and place....

"Has your family been in America a long time?" Norman asks the boy.

"Yeah. I don't know. Yeah." The boy's braces gleam in the fluorescent light. Then he adds, "My grandpa was in the army. He showed me his uniform once."

"The American army?"

"Sure." Norman looks slightly relieved. Later, he says, "The boy looked like such a German."

I ask if he still likes his new friend, and he replies, "Of course. You can't hold such things against people. It's not his fault. He's just a boy."

The event is over, and Norman seems tired but energized at the same time. He has done his duty.

I need to catch a flight to the airport, and Norman insists on driving me, although the traffic will be heavy and it will not be a pleasant drive. However, it gives us time to talk in the car. I take out my pen and notebook and scramble to write as fast as he talks, thankful for the old-timers in the newspaper business who some years ago taught me a form of shorthand.

"You know, my wife says that I was spoiled by women when I was a child. Okay! Okay! So it is true! Who wouldn't be spoiled? I had five older sisters. One of them, I even called Mama until I was three or four years old."

Norman explains that he was the youngest of nine children; his mother, whose name was Esther, was forty years old when he was born. The oldest child, his brother Avrum (Albert), was twenty years older than Norman and left for America before he was born. Another brother, David, went to Palestine. That left at home only one brother, Leibush, who was sixteen years older—and the five sisters, for whom, to hear Norman tell it, he was a pampered pet.

I love to hear these stories. He is smiling, and I am smiling. It is not hard for me to picture Norman, whose name was actually Naftali, as a spoiled little mischief maker with five doting older sisters. The dynamics would likely be the same in any family—Jewish or Christian, black or white.

Norman's hazel eyes become more lively when he talks about his childhood. How he loved his hometown, Kolbuszowa. His family, as he describes it, was better off than most of the Jews in the town because his father, Izak, owned a successful store, a general wholesale store where you could find most anything you might need. The family name was Saleschutz, and they were very observant Jews known as Hasidim. Many of the women wore long skirts and shawls, although Norman says his sisters did not. Men usually wore black kapotas, black velour hats, and had long beards and earlocks. In Norman's family, he and his brothers followed the custom until they were about fourteen or fifteen years old.

Norman's father had been the only one of seven brothers and sisters who did not go to America in the 1880s. "He was the most religious, and he felt that if he left Kolbuszowa and went to America, he would not be able to raise his children in the traditional way," Norman says. He adds, "My father wanted me to become a religious scholar. My older brothers disappointed him, and he pinned all his hopes on me. Oh, well! I am afraid I let him down, too."

There was a long tradition of scholarly Judaism in Norman's family. In fact, his grandfather (his mother's father) was a gifted and famed scholar named Leibush Avrumalis-Berl. This esteemed ancestor wrote a book in 1875 called *Yehoshua Hanotzri* or *Jesus of Nazareth*.

Norman shakes his head sadly. "I would give up all my possessions to see that book again. Imagine! A scholarly Jew who studied and wrote about Jesus! It was—how would you say?—an oddity, a curiosity. You know, my father used to hide that book in his study. It is long gone, destroyed in the war."

Life, as Norman remembers it, was simple but good. There was no electricity in Kolbuszowa. The town was not even on a railroad line. Transportation meant taking the bus that came through town or riding in wagons pulled by horses or walking on your own two feet.

The most important part of Jewish life, Norman says, was to live thoughtfully and purposefully. Following the dictates of Judaism, Norman's father allowed the poor and elderly to accept food and other items from the store. They would pay him back if they could. If they couldn't, nothing was ever said about it.

"The performing of charity, this is called *Tzedakah*, and it is a very important part of Judaism," Norman instructs me, taking one hand off the wheel to emphasize the point. Norman's comments make me realize how little I know about Judaism, although my own religion, Christianity, is derived from it.

Amalie told me earlier that Norman does not talk often about his sisters and rarely in any detail. And so I press him here for some specifics. Who were they? What were their names? What were they like?

The oldest sister's name was Bluma-Gela, named after his father's mother. She was, he says, called Gela. She was seventeen years older than Norman. When Gela got married, she and her new husband moved into two rooms on the second floor of her parents' house but "ended up staying there for twenty years!" Norman says with a laugh. Gela's husband was a well-regarded scholar from Cracow named Ruben Weinstein, a grandchild of one of the most famous Hasidic rabbis, Santzer Rabbi Chaim Halberstam.

Ruben had no trade, so Norman's father set him up selling textiles. Gela and Ruben had one daughter, Shandel Matl, named after Norman's mother's mother. "We called her Shandel. She was three years younger than me, and I grew up with her like another sister. She was a very good student, and she had the most beautiful voice, which she got from her father.

"After Gela was my brother Leibush, who I will tell you more about later," Norman says. He is on a roll now. "Then came my sister Alte Malka. She was named after my mother's sister, who died at age twenty-eight giving birth to her fifth child."

Norman explains that it was the Jewish custom to name children in memory of a family member who had died. Alte, which means "old" in Yiddish, was added when the person after whom the child was named was young at the time of her death. (Alte was added for girls, Alter for boys. Or sometimes Chaya, which means "life," was added for girls, Chaim for boys.)

"Slow down, Norman, this is confusing," I protest, but he keeps talking. "Anyway, for short we called Alte Malka by the name Malcia. Okay, so you want to know about Malcia. Well, she was altogether different than Gela. *Malka* means 'queen' in Hebrew, and that is what she was! I think she was the prettiest one of all my sisters. She was born in 1907; she was already thirteen when I was born."

Which one did he call "Mama"?

"Oh, that was Malcia! She pampered me the most. When the Gypsies came through town, she would run and get me at the Jewish school and take me to see them performing tricks. Then my father would find out from the teacher that I was taken from school, and he would say to Malcia, 'How can you do that? He's missing his lessons.'"

It wasn't hard for the local matchmaker to find young men who were interested in the Saleschutz girls, Norman tells me. "They were smart and pretty girls, and not only that, they had a pretty good dowry—equal to about two thousand American dollars, while five hundred dollars was typical."

The matchmaker arranged for Malcia to meet a man named Szaye David Lische from Dembica, a grandson of a famous rabbi from Dynow, and the young couple agreed to marry. Malcia also really never left home, according to Norman. It seems the newlyweds lived with them for about a year, and then Norman's father bought the house next door for them.

Szaye David was a Talmudic scholar. "He had no trade, so my father gave him part of our business—the flour part of our business. He developed it himself and made a good living.

"Malcia and her husband did not have children right away and were very happy when finally they had a little girl named Bluma-Gela," Norman says, pausing to spell it for me. "Since we already had a Bluma-Gela in the family, we called this little one Blimcia." Born in 1938, Blimcia had blonde, curly hair and "blue eyes like water," Norman says. "Every time I went somewhere I never came back without a chocolate or an apple or a pear, not just for Blimcia, who would be waiting for me, but for all the children. They were like my children because we all lived together." Malcia and her husband had a second daughter, Dobcia, in 1940.

Norman's third sister was Lieba Ryfka, born in 1909 and named after his mother's grandmother. "She was a very gentle person, very devoted to the family," Norman says quietly. Then he brightens. "There is a family story that one time Lieba was seen running down the street with a piece of bread in her hand, crying. People asked her, 'Why are you crying?' And she replied that I had run away and wouldn't eat my bread! I guess I was three or four years old. You see how spoiled I was?"

He laughs at himself and then appears lost in thought for a moment. "Did I tell you about the dance lessons?"

Dance lessons?

"We were all fascinated by America, and at one point a dance instructor came to Kolbuszowa who knew how to teach American dances. It was too expensive for all of my five sisters to take the class, so Lieba is the one, she took lessons and taught the others. Every Saturday in our house, especially in the winter when it was cold and snowy, we had our own dance class! We didn't have music because first, we didn't have a gramophone, and second, on Saturday you couldn't use a gramophone because it was forbidden [on the Sabbath]. So who did the music? I did! I knew the melodies, and I remember them until today. From the time I was eight until I was about twelve, I learned those dances. I remember the shimmy and the Szarleston [Charleston] even now."

"Your father," I ask, surprised, "allowed that?"

"My father was religious, but he wasn't so strict that he forbade us from having good times," Norman replies. "Okay, so where was I? Oh, yes, Lieba. She got married in 1937 to a man named Moses Kornfeld, a student at Yeshiva Chachmei Lublin, a very prestigious yeshiva [school for higher learning]. Unlike my other sisters' husbands, he spoke very good Polish. Lieba was envied that she got herself such a husband."

46

Once again, the newlyweds spent a year at the home of the bride's parents—until the bride's father bought them a house and set up his son-in-law in business, in this case, the wholesale textile business. Lieba was especially devoted to her mother, helping out back at "home" even when she had her own children—Henech, a son born in 1938, and a second son, Josef, born in 1940.

"It sounds like life was pretty close to perfect," I say, still scribbling away frantically and making a note to check all these spellings later.

Norman's mood seems to have changed, and I wonder what he is thinking. It flashes through my mind that he might be thinking, *Yeah, life was pretty close to perfect. Until those evil-blooded German people came along.* But apparently, I'm wrong.

"We had a tragedy during those years, a very sad thing that affected the whole family," Norman says. I wait for him to say more. "Josef, Lieba's baby, was blind. When he was eight days old, he was circumcised, and after that, he got yellow jaundice. I don't know if it was related to the circumcision or not. Anyway, we knew he should see a doctor immediately, but there was no doctor because this was during German occupation. Josef was a beautiful little boy, and it was very sad for the whole family because, you see, my family was the type of people who loved children. We put the children first. The children first."

Norman sighs and says something like, "Ehhh," and shakes his head sadly, as if to shake off the memory. And I am thinking, *Poor innocent child.*

Norman clears his throat and goes on. "Did I tell you about Matl? She was the fourth sister. Actually, her name was Matl Shandel. She was born in 1911. She was an altogether different type. All the sisters were different! Matl was very intelligent, spoke beautiful Hebrew, and was the first one of the sisters to belong to a Zionist organization, Hanoar Hatzioni [Young Zionists]."

What else? What else can you tell me about her?

Norman laughs suddenly. "Matl was a very good student, but she didn't bother with anything in the house. She didn't know how to make a cup of tea! But she took over the business from my father, writing down customer orders, taking care of the bills, and at night she was the bookkeeper. She was funny. When I was tiny, I remember that she used to grab me and kiss me, and I would run away, so sometimes when she caught me, she would bite me."

Matl is the one who introduced Norman to the movies, not something a boy attending religious school was supposed to be exposed to. "Matl liked to bring me along because I loved it so much and she couldn't refuse me anything, but if I were caught going to a movie, I would be thrown out from my religious school," Norman says. "So what she and my other sisters did was to tie up my earlocks under a beret to make me look like a girl!"

What movies did they see? "Oh, everything from Hollywood. Our favorites were movies with stars like Jeanette MacDonald, Nelson Eddy, and Charlie Chaplin. Whenever I saw a movie, I would say to myself, 'Someday I will be there! I will be part of it! In America!'"

Did Matl get married?

"No," Norman says, although before the war, "the matchmakers started to come and talk to Matl, and she used to go to different towns to look over boys. I remember my father always said that once he got Matl married, she would take over our businesses and he would visit America and see the World's Fair [1939]."

Neither event ever happened.

There is one more sister to hear about, and we're getting close to the airport where Norman will drop me off. "Tell me about the last one," I say, recognizing that he is on a roll and, for all I know, won't want to return to this topic another day.

"Okay, the fifth sister, the one closest to me in age, was Reisel Rachel. She was born in 1917. She was called Rechla. Put together the best of all of the sisters, and that was Rechla! She was very pretty, very intelligent; there did not seem to be a boy in Kolbuszowa who was not in love with her. Everyone said she looked like Ingrid Bergman. She became a leader of Hanoar Hatzioni, the Zionist organization. She spoke beautiful Hebrew, Polish, German, Yiddish, eventually even English. She was already different from the other sisters because she went out with boys on dates."

Rechla had something of a stormy love life, it seems. One young man she was close to, Norman tells me, made the mistake of going away to Jerusalem to study. While he was gone, another young man pursued Rechla, Norman says, and they became engaged. Their plan was to go to America, and they struggled to get proper papers.

It did not work out as the young couple had hoped. "He managed to get out one week before war broke out, but my sister remained stranded in Poland," Norman says sadly. For quite a while, he adds, the young pair managed to send love letters through a distant cousin of the Saleschutz family in Switzerland. "It was heartbreaking to see how much she loved him and missed him. As it turned out, she never saw him again."

Another sad tale, dreams deferred, hopes crushed. The victims of the war are starting to take shape for me now, beyond mere numbers. They are faces now; they are individuals with unique stories.

"There is something else I have to tell you," Norman says

in a voice that makes me sit up straight. "There was a girl, her name was Rozia Susskind, and I wanted to marry her. I had my eye on Rozia since I was maybe ten or twelve years old, but Hassidic Jewish boys were not allowed to mix with girls so I had to wait years before I finally approached her. The way I finally got to know her was that I joined the Hanoar Hatzioni and took over from my sister Rechla. And Rozia, she joined, too. She became my girlfriend, and our dream was to get married and to go to Palestine."

Rozia was not from a family that was as religious as the Saleschutz clan, but she was accepted anyway. "All my family loved Rozia because I loved her!" Norman exclaims.

Norman was just becoming a young man, and his sisters were young women—the older ones married with small children—when the war broke out. In many ways, they lived much like their ancestors had lived for many generations. They had no reason to believe that would change so radically.

Norman looks tired now. It has been a long day. There's a lot more to say, but it will have to wait for another day. We have arrived at our destination, Newark International Airport. Norman navigates the circuitous route to the airport terminal, slamming on the brakes at crucial moments and yelling at other drivers. "Okay, taxi man, go first if you must!" He mutters something in Polish under his breath. Although he seems agitated, paradoxically, he seems to be enjoying himself. He is a warrior, after all.

As I say thank you and good-bye at the curb, my mind is spinning with images of life in Kolbuszowa, Poland, a place I had never even heard of, but now is coming to life in my heart.

Chapter Five

A PREMONITION

nother week passes. I am back from my plane trip, a brief respite from the intensity of being with Norman and Amalie. However, something peculiar has happened: I wasn't really able to get away from it. Norman's and Amalie's stories are on my mind during my waking hours and even at night in my dreams.

For some inexplicable reason I have been particularly obsessed with the story of Celia, Amalie's younger sister. I am not a crier, yet Celia has moved me to tears in my office as I listen to my tape recordings and review my notes.

It is time for another visit to the cream-colored house in Springfield, New Jersey. I tell Amalie how Celia has really gotten under my skin.

"Perhaps it is because Celia was young and innocent, and she reminds you of your nieces," Amalie suggests, referring to my older brother's daughters, Anna and Barbara Hill, who happen to be that age.

We pick up where we left off in our last conversation. Norman is not home; he is out giving his talk to another community group, this time at a library.

The weather is cooler now so we will talk at the cozy kitchen table. It is hard to get Amalie to settle down and focus because her instinct to take care of her guest—"What would you like to eat? How about a banana? How about some chocolates? Have you had your yogurt today? What about your orange juice?"—prevails.

"You don't have to fuss over me like this," I protest, knowing it's futile.

"I can't help it. I am a Jewish mother," she says, smiling. "I know you have a mother, but now you also know what it's like to have a Jewish mother!"

Amalie at last is seated. Taking out my notes, I say, "Now where were we?" I'm trying to make it easy for her to start anywhere she wants to.

Once again, I find that Amalie bravely gets right to the point. "I want to tell you that after Celia was taken away, my mother's chestnut hair turned completely white. Completely white, overnight! And just forty-one years old."

Amalie explains how she felt during this time. Although just a teenager herself, she says she thought she was somehow responsible for her parents. Pepka, the elder sister, was safe in Palestine. Celia was gone. And Amalie, suddenly rushed into an adult world, tried to "be strong, to comfort" her parents.

Her father, who had served dutifully in the Austrian army during World War I, felt doubly betrayed. He was shocked that the Germans would murder a young girl, that they had no remorse or regret, that no one cared, that there was to be no inquiry, nothing. How could they do this to his daughter, the child of a veteran?

"It made no sense, but then we were just at the beginning of an era when nothing made sense anymore," Amalie says simply.

And so her sister lay in an unmarked mass grave somewhere in the Polish countryside. The Petranker family never learned exactly where it was located. After a while, there would be so many other mass graves that it would not be possible to tell one from another.

Amalie explains to me that the mayhem seemed to originate with little things, small indignities, until their rights as citizens were stripped away.

"We were not allowed in certain stores. We could not walk on the sidewalk, only in the street. It grew from there until it reached the point where people were killed outright, like Celia."

In fact, on the very day of Celia's disappearance, as Amalie ran home, she witnessed two German soldiers harass, then shoot and kill an older Jewish man on the sidewalk.

The world had indeed gone mad. Yet there was more, much more, to come.

"One night not long after Celia's disappearance," Amalie tells me, "I was awakened by my mother. She came to my bed and sat down and put her arms around me. I was alarmed by this because my mother was a sweet and gentle woman, but she was not especially affectionate, not like this. She held onto me and wept. It was very frightening for me. I said, 'Mother, you must have been dreaming.' After a while, we both went back to sleep."

Later, Amalie realized it was not a dream. It was more like a premonition. Her mother was saying good-bye.

For weeks, as the Jewish high holy days approached, there was great tension throughout Stanislawow, Amalie recalls. The Germans had devised a plan to move the Jews into a ghetto, just as they were doing in many other cities in Europe. David Petranker found a tiny apartment in the area within the ghetto's boundaries, in case the family needed to move there. There were many rumors, and it was, as Amalie recalls, anyone's guess which ones were valid.

Amalie asks me if I have ever known such fear, and I say, no, and I hope I never do.

"I hope you don't, either," she says.

One day a friend of David Petranker's, a musician who was forced to play in a Jewish band that performed for German officers, reported that the Gestapo chief, a man named Krueger, had made the musicians perform for a week at the Jewish cemetery while Jews were ordered to dig large trenches there. What on earth was it all about? The most optimistic among them theorized that perhaps it meant that the Germans were retreating from the Russian front and were preparing new defense lines. Maybe the Germans were losing the war! The other possibility was unthinkable.

And then it happened.

It was October 12, 1941, the day of Hoshanah Rabba (the seventh day of the Jewish holiday Sukkoth), one of the Jewish high holy days. Amalie tells it to me this way:

"A few hours after my mother had awakened me with her strange dream, we all suddenly jumped out of our beds because of a strange rumbling noise coming from the street. We ran to the balcony and saw hundreds of German and Ukrainian policemen and many—I don't know how many—canvas-covered trucks and other vehicles."

What they thought was happening, she says, was that the Germans might be coming after them in the same way they did the Hungarian Jews. They kidnapped the men, took them from their families, turned the men into slave laborers, and left the families behind to starve. Guessing that was about to happen to them, Amalie and her mother hid David Petranker in the attic.

"Outside, the Germans were yelling, *'Juden heraus! Juden heraus!'* (Jews get out! Jews get out!) A neighbor, a fourteen-year-old Jewish boy named Lonek Richter, suddenly knocked on the door and cried out, 'Aren't you going to hide? Aren't you going to hide?'"

Amalie's hands are trembling as she speaks.

So are mine.

"Our young friend Lonek told us that people were going to hide in the cellar. We gathered in the hallway, trying to decide what to do. The houses on our block were joined together; that is common in many European cities. Each home had its own attic and cellar, but they were interconnected. It was agreed. We would all go to the cellar and hide there."

So, your father was in the attic, and you and your mother went to the cellar with the others?

"No," she says. "I do not know why, but I refused. I told the others that if the Germans come inside the buildings that I believed they would search the cellars first. My mother tried to persuade me, but I could not be convinced to change my mind. One older woman chose to stay with me; the rest went to the cellar."

Amalie and the older woman locked themselves in the last room of the Petranker family's apartment. The noise from the streets continued all day. At one point, Lonek, the young boy, came to the door with a message from her mother, asking her to change her mind, but she was determined to stay.

"By evening, the streets began to get quiet, and the older woman and I snuck out of the back room to look around. At the staircase in our building, we ran into a Catholic couple who lived in our building. They were shocked to see us."

"Dear God, you are still here?" the woman cried. She told Amalie and the older woman that at about three o'clock, the Gestapo had come into the building. Led by a young Polish Catholic boy—the son of a neighbor—the Germans were taken straight to the cellar where the young boy knew the Jews were hiding.

"Betrayed again," I say very softly to myself. "For no reason at all except hate."

Amalie hears me. "Yes, this is true. For no reason at all except hate."

So what happened next?

The entire group, the Catholic couple told them, had been loaded onto a truck and taken to the Jewish cemetery.

"When I heard the word *cemetery*, I nearly fainted," Amalie says, putting her hand to her heart unconsciously. "I ran up to the attic and called my father's name. 'Mother was taken away!' I cried. After I was able to get him out of the attic—we had locked him in there—I collapsed in my father's arms, crying on his shoulder."

Father and daughter sat huddled together in the apartment, numbed by what had happened. "Perhaps she is wounded and trying to find her way home," David Petranker said hopefully at one point. "Perhaps I should go look for her."

But Amalie said, no, we must stay put.

Later that evening, there was a knock at the door. It was Yetta Richter, young Lonek's mother. The poor woman was an eyewitness to the day's events at the cemetery. She had survived and found her way home. Hysterical, she somehow managed to come tell them what had taken place.

Amalie, trancelike, continues to tell me in her own words:

"In the truck, on the ride to the cemetery, she said that Frieda Petranker had continually spoken of how she should have listened to her daughter. When they arrived at the cemetery, the area was surrounded by Ukrainian militia. German soldiers were posted with machine guns at several locations. There was a square building inside the cemetery, where several Gestapo men with machine guns stood guard. A row of machine guns was lined up at one end of the cemetery, on one side of a row of long, deep pits—the pits dug previously by Jews, as my father's musician friend had warned us. As they were unloaded from the trucks, the Jews were told to put their hands behind their heads and march to the back of the cemetery.

"The entire operation was overseen by Krueger, chief of the Gestapo in our area, a tall, blond man in his midthirties. He sent a group of young Jewish girls with baskets to collect watches, jewelry, coins, and other valuables. German and Ukrainian guards pushed people with their rifle butts in the first row, forcing them to line up in front of the pits. All was quiet except for the sound of some people who were mumbling prayers. Then Krueger shot the Jew standing closest to him, the signal for the machine guns to start firing.

"Row after row, the Jews fell into the pits. Krueger was a madman. He shot some Jews himself at close range. As row after row was prodded forward, some tried to flee or fought back but were killed instantly. Others, realizing what was happening, struggled toward the back. A number of them survived because once the trenches were full and it began to get dark, the Germans told those who were left alive to go home."

And what happened to her mother?

Amalie pauses, collecting herself. "Our neighbor, Mrs. Richter, told us that my mother, too, might have survived in this way. But she was unable to endure waiting her turn to be killed, and she actually ran toward the front."

Ran toward the front—I wonder what I would do in that situation. Perhaps the same thing. Get it over with.

As it turned out, Frieda Petranker, forty-one years old, was one of twelve thousand Jews murdered there on that day.

And young Lonek, Mrs. Richter's son?

"He perished also," Amalie says softly.

David Petranker was filled with remorse and regrets, saying that he should have let Amalie leave with the count. But,

Amalie recalls with something close to pride, "I told him I'd rather be with him, no matter what."

He began to cry, she says, and agreed. "Yes, Manya, we will stay together," he replied, using the name he always called Amalie. "This is what a family does. Whatever happens to one will happen to us both."

Amalie dabs at her eyes with a tissue. Almost sixty years have passed, but the time vanishes. "My poor father. And my poor mother—oh, I really loved them," she says. "I wish I could go back in time and fix things, change things somehow, but I cannot."

There is nothing to say or do but just sit here as the words hang in the air. I am thinking, *I wish the Holocaust deniers could sit in my place and hear these stories. To look into someone's eyes and listen is to experience it—not firsthand, of course, but nevertheless in a deep, empathetic, and very personal way. When you hold someone's hand and it trembles, her sorrows have become yours. This is true even if you say nothing, for sometimes there are no words.*

A few days later, I am on an Amtrak Express train bound from New York to Washington, headed to the United States Holocaust Memorial Museum.

"You have to go," Norman and Amalie had told me.

"I do?" I said meekly, hoping to postpone the inevitable. They were right, of course; I could not write this book without going. Thankfully, my husband, Blair, offered to go with me.

I try to put Norman and Amalie out of my mind for a few hours on the train, but it does not seem possible; and as Blair dozes my mind wanders. Even the New Jersey and Pennsylvania countryside, seen from the train window, reminds me of Norman and Amalie. In my mind's eye, I could be looking at the Polish countryside of the 1930s and

1940s, the way Norman and Amalie describe it. Cows and horses meander through fields as burly men toss hay with pitchforks.

But interspersed with vistas of stunning countryside are scenes of urban tragedy, America's great shame. Seen fleetingly from the window of the speeding train, the people of inner-city Trenton, Philadelphia, Baltimore, and Washington look trapped and defeated. They walk slowly, their heads hung low. I can't help thinking that they are the spiritual counterparts of the Jews in the ghettos of Europe during the German occupation.

The doors of the museum open at 10:00 A.M., and by 9:30 already a long line of visitors wait patiently. My plan is to go unannounced, not as a journalist but as an anonymous tourist with my husband. The crowd is well-behaved, quiet, and thoughtful. Americans in jeans talk quietly among themselves. Languages other than English are easy to overhear including, on this morning, French, Italian, Japanese, and Russian. I've been told all my life that I look very German, so I'm feeling a little self-conscious. Then I scold myself for feeling that way: *For pete's sake, you're an American. These feelings are ridiculous.*

The children's exhibit beckons across the atrium. Perhaps this is a good place to start. Called "Remember the Children: Daniel's Story," it attracts people of all ages. The exhibit tells the story of a boy named Daniel, a survivor who loses his mother and sister. "Daniel" narrates his story as visitors walk through the experiential display, through his "home," his family's quarters in the ghetto, and finally a glimpse of concentration camp life, gently censored.

Children are encouraged to express their feelings by writing postcards to Daniel. Paper and colored pens are left invitingly on a long table. Some results are affixed to the wall above for everyone to contemplate. Several of them catch my eye:

A painting of a black barbed-wire fence with a blue teardrop superimposed over it. In small letters at the bottom are the words *I'm sad, too*.

Another painting depicts a sad face behind bars with the word *terrible* in bold black letters across the top. Near it is one that says simply, "Sorry," in green block letters. Yet another says, "I am sorry that the Germans could do something this terrible to other human beings, especially since I am half German."

Whoa, my feelings exactly.

The museum is designed to give one a chance to think and to feel. It is time to face the main exhibit. "God," I pray silently, "help me get through this." A respectful crowd lines up near the entrance, and Blair and I quietly join them. A museum guide points to a table with a huge pile of identical-looking "ID cards," each one a small folder containing a name, photograph, and vital statistics of a Holocaust victim. As the crowd passes by, each person takes an ID card at random. The intention, a volunteer explains, is to make the experience more personal by reminding visitors that each victim was an individual.

I don't even look at my ID card immediately, but when I open it, I'm so shocked I let out a yelp. Blair looks alarmed as I grab his arm. The security guards move closer.

By sheer and amazing coincidence, the ID card that I randomly grabbed from the midst of the pile is that of Celia Petranker.

Celia Petranker? Amalie's sister, Celia! The logical side of me could not believe my eyes.

"What are the chances of picking any one ID card on a given day?" I ask some workers standing nearby, once I have collected myself. They seem surprised by the question. "I don't know," says an older man. "Why do you ask?"

I show him the ID card and explain what has happened. He confers with a few other workers and volunteers, and after some discussion, they agree that this is an extraordinary occurrence. I am glad that Blair was with me to share the experience.

I feel exhilarated. With Celia's ID card clutched tightly in my hand, I am now fortified and ready to face the main exhibit. How could I not, with Celia leading the way for me?

Most of the visitors, including myself, are unescorted by a tour guide and simply follow their own pace. Out of curiosity, I decide to trail a German-speaking family, a husband and wife with a teenage son and daughter. My knowledge of German is poor, but it is not hard to interpret their feelings. Like everyone else, they look awed and overwhelmed, sad and thoughtful. The one difference is that the German-speaking family look self-conscious.

At one point they look directly at me. The husband smiles and suddenly asks me something in German.

Oh, great, he thinks I'm one of them.

"Nein," I reply. "No sprechen sie Deutsch." He looks surprised.

At the end of the exhibit, they look more haggard than those around them. They disappear into the crowd, speaking to no one, not even each other.

Leaving the building is like returning to the surface after swimming underwater. Suddenly, you can breathe again. In the outside world, the world of "now," it is a beautiful day. A man is selling Polish sausage, of all things, from a pushcart in front of the museum. No one is buying. The smell of it makes me sick.

I keep walking, relieved to be back in my world. It's

exhilarating! Good old Washington, D.C., seems like a familiar friend. Within sight of the Lincoln Memorial, I join a group of tourists who pause to observe a man dressed in a business suit; he holds an enormous hand-painted sign that reads, "Impeach Clinton!" Some passersby sneer; others cheer him on. But no one attempts to harm him. Better yet, no one arrests him. He is not beaten or dragged away by the Gestapo, never to be seen again.

Down the block, an older woman tosses pieces of bread to hungry pigeons who appear to be her only companions. A policeman walking by pauses and asks if she has a place to sleep that night. Satisfied with her response, he smiles and goes on his way.

I watch these scenes through new eyes. My thought processes have changed in the last few hours. The U.S. Holocaust Memorial Museum, I realize, is as much a tribute to democracy as it is to the failings of humankind.

That night, back at my hotel room, I call Norman and Amalie on the phone. I want to share the experience of randomly choosing the ID of one Celia Petranker.

"You must have screamed!" Norman says. Then thoughtfully, joyfully, he adds: "It must be that your God and our God got together and decided to make that happen."

Amalie picks up the phone extension in the kitchen, and I repeat the story to her. "It is unbelievable," she says, her voice heavy with emotion. "I think this is what they call a miracle."

Chapter Six

A LONG HISTORY

Norman is weary. It is a few weeks after his visit to the school in Garwood. He is limping a bit and, after lunch, finds it difficult to navigate the stairs down to his recreation-room office from the kitchen.

"See that," Amalie says worriedly. "He can hardly walk today. Do you know why? Because he is stubborn, that is why. He listens to no one."

Norman continues his descent to his office retreat. "Yeah, yeah, yeah," he says wearily. "It'll be better tomorrow."

"Norman forgets he is an old man," Amalie says.

When it is suggested that seventy-eight isn't really all that old, Amalie shakes her head. "That is true for Americans who have lived here all their lives. It is not true for someone who has been through what Norman and I have been through."

Norman has reached the bottom of the half-flight of stairs and calls out, "Ho, ho, but I'm a tough old bird."

In most households there is a struggle of wills. In the Salsitz home, the battle seems to be who will get the last word.

Amalie settles in at the kitchen table with her newspaper. "You see, he was outside yesterday all day long, supervising the men who put in our new fence. As if the men couldn't do it themselves. He wore himself out, and I'm sure he wore those men out, too. Now his knee is bothering him today. I went out and told him, 'Norman, you shouldn't be standing

63

around all day like this; it's not good for you,' but he doesn't listen to me."

Norman's version of the event is somewhat different. "Those men needed me," he insists. "After all, I'm the one who put in the original fence forty years ago. Who would know better than I how it should be done, to put in a new one? I'd have done it myself, but my wife wouldn't let me. So we paid these men so much money, an incredible amount of money, and they did it, but they needed my help. That's the way it is these days. You pay them a lot of money, and you still have to do it yourself, you know."

But what about that sore knee?

"Oh, that's nothing," he says. "Just a little arthritis. Look," he says, holding out his hands. "I've got all kinds of little problems. See this finger?" he asks, flexing the pointer finger on his right hand. "A bullet went through there. Right through it! Sometimes, when it's cold, I can't move it at all. Someday I'll die, but for now I just keep on going."

This leads to another thought. "When I die, I'm going to be buried here in New Jersey," he muses. "When I first came to America, I bought a couple of burial plots—that's where we'll end up."

It is meant to be a pragmatic comment, but is a sad one. There is no old family plot, not here, not anywhere. Not anymore. Displaced and torn from their motherland in life, they are also homeless in death. Norman, in particular, had anticipated as a child that someday he would be buried alongside his ancestors in the Jewish cemetery in Kolbuszowa. It was part of the expected rhythm of life.

But these lives—his and Amalie's—have not taken their natural course. In some ways they remind me of people I've met as a journalist over the years, ordinary people who leave for work one morning and return home to find their world upended by a flood, earthquake, fire, or accident. For Norman and Amalie, there is the same sense of disbelief, shock, anger, and grief.

People who survive an accident or natural disaster, however, can stand and rail at the gods and shake a fist in fury. For Amalie and Norman, it is far more complex.

Sometimes, Norman's way of dealing with his anger is to tell a joke. Today, he has a new one for me:

"One day a Christian man said to a Jew, 'You know, you Jews are responsible for everything bad that happens.'

"The Jew said, 'Like what?'

"And the Christian gave a long list of outrageous things, ending the list with the sinking of the *Titanic*.

" 'What?' said the Jew. 'You are crazy! What did we have to do with the sinking of the *Titanic*?'

" 'It was caused by an iceberg,' the Christian replied.

" 'An iceberg?' the Jew asked incredulously.

" 'Iceberg, Greenberg, what's the difference, he was a Jew,' said the Christian."

Norman laughs at his own joke, a hearty laugh, but then becomes serious. He wants me to understand.

"That is how it sometimes feels to be a Jew in this world," he says. "The funny thing is, Jesus was a Jew. He was a good Jewish boy! Christianity is an offspring of Judaism. We share many of the same teachings and principles. Why don't we appreciate that more?"

Norman adds that when he was a boy, he would hear Polish Christians say that Jews were "Christ killers." Never mind, Norman adds defensively, that the Jews didn't kill Jesus Christ; the Romans did.

Another thing that was said about Jews, Norman tells me, was that they "snatched Christian children and drank their blood." There are many accounts, which I learned in my research, indicating that many Polish Christians believed this was true.

Norman wants to make clear to me that the Holocaust did not spring out of nowhere, caused by one evil man, Adolf Hitler. "There was such deep hatred of Jews throughout Europe, going back two thousand years. This was how the Holocaust was possible. This hatred was worse in some places than others. In Poland, it was particularly bad. Nine out of ten Polish Jews did not survive World War II."

Where did this hatred stem from?

"Part of it was that the Polish people were mostly very poor, and there was much jealousy. Many Jewish families sacrificed to get the best education possible for their children. Often, young Jews went elsewhere, such as Germany [before Hitler], Italy, France, Czechoslovakia, or sometimes Britain, for advanced degrees and returned home to Poland where they often became top in their fields. This caused a lot of resentment."

Jews were not usually able to get government jobs in Poland, Norman points out. As a result, Jews had to go into business for themselves to survive. "Then people turned around and complained that we had too much power, that we were greedy, that we owned too much," Norman says with an incredulous shrug of the shoulders. "All we did was work hard, and this was held against us.

"Have you ever heard the expression, 'I'm going to Jew him down?'" Norman asks, and I'm embarrassed to admit that yes, I have heard it. "It means that the person is going to try to lower the price of something by arguing with the shop-keeper," Norman says. "But it is a mean-spirited distortion of the Jewish tradition of negotiating for the price of an item you wish to buy."

There is something else that Norman seems a little reluc-tant to bring up. Perhaps he does not wish to hurt my feelings. But I've already read a lot about it during my visit to the Holocaust Museum: the troubling fact that anti-Semitism in Poland was encouraged, over the centuries, by the church.

Gently, he tells me that this is "sad but true, and I saw it with my own eyes. I heard it with my own ears."

As an example, Norman tells me this story:

"I knew a Polish Catholic woman named Mary Drazek who worked for a Jewish man and was well treated and well paid and very happy in her job, but her parish priest told her she must quit. She should not work for a Jew is what he said. She refused, and the priest said that if she did not quit, she would not be allowed to take Communion or to be buried in the church cemetery. This was fairly typical, this kind of threat. In this case, she was young and rebellious, and she simply left for America."

According to Norman, Jews were not accepted in Poland even after living there for some six hundred years. Jews had lived in Kolbuszowa for about three hundred years, yet they were treated "like unwanted newcomers," he says.

How many Jews and how many Christians lived in Kolbuszowa?

Norman estimates that when he was a young boy, of four thousand residents of the town, half were Jews and half were Christians. The two groups lived in separate parts of town. Most of the time they lived in peace, but a minor incident, misunderstanding, or even the most ridiculous rumor could set off violence at any time, he recalls.

The periodic attacks were known among the Jews as pogroms. One of the worst pogroms in Kolbuszowa's history happened on May 6, 1919, one year to the day before Norman was born. Records indicate that 9 Jews were murdered, 45 young Jewish girls were raped (among them a ten-year-old girl who became mentally ill and stayed that way until she was killed by the Germans in 1942), and 250 Jews were wounded. In addition, virtually every Jewish home was robbed or damaged.

This event was locally famous, but it was not remembered with shame and condemnation. Rather, Norman says, it was *celebrated* for many years afterward. "When I was a young boy, I often heard Polish boys singing about that day," Norman says dryly. "They changed the words to a famous patriotic song, like this."

> Mazurka of the Third of May
> Welcome, the May dawn, shine upon our country,
> We shall honor you with a song, play, and wine,
> Welcome May, beautiful May, for the Poles a blissful paradise!

After the pogrom, the words were sometimes altered:

> The third of May, the sixth of May, break the windows of the Jews,
> Beat the Jews, kill the Jews, for the Poles a blissful paradise!

Christian boys sang this in the streets, he recalls. In fact, he knew many of the boys. Although Jews and Christians lived separately, Jewish and Christian boys sat side by side at public school. Privately educated in religious studies, together they learned such subjects as math and history in Polish at public school.

Anti-Semitism was so commonplace that even the public school teachers were open about it, Norman recalls. "Once, when I was in second grade, I had a Christian teacher who cornered the Hasidic boys and cut off the earlocks of every one he could get his hands on!" Norman exclaims, still indignant over the episode these many years later. "Some of the boys cried as the hair fell to the floor. When he came at me with those scissors, I ran away. I jumped over some desks and pushed past a teacher who was helping by blocking the doorway. I ran all the way home screaming my head

68

off. My father was furious and took the matter to the authorities, but in the end the whole thing was dropped. Nothing came of it."

Norman is silent for a moment, but telling me the incident sparks a memory far more painful. The only time he ever saw his father cry, he says, involved a similar incident.

"After the Germans were in charge, in 1939, they kept coming up with new rules and regulations that were intended to hurt us little by little," Norman says wearily. "One day there was a rule that all Jewish men must shave their beards. Well, to someone like my father, this was a violation of biblical law. He had never cut his beard in his entire adult life! The barber assigned by the Germans came to our house, and after he shaved off my father's beard, I saw that my father was a changed man. I saw tears in his eyes. All he said was, 'Now I have felt the taste of death.'"

More than a physical assault, the act was clearly designed to destroy dignity, pride, and identity. "It was supposed to break us, but with me it did the opposite: I vowed to fight back. I thought, *I'm going to live through this and find a better world.*"

He turns to a joke to lighten the moment: "You could say I am resilient. Of course, my wife, she would say I am stubborn!"

Call it persistence, defiance, resilience, or yes, even stubbornness, it is clear that both Norman and Amalie had what it takes to escape the Holocaust.

"I'm always aware that they've been through a lot, and it amazes me," their longtime neighbor, Gerald Yablonsky, tells me. A retired teacher and administrator in the Newark public schools, Mr. Yablonsky moved into the house directly across the street from Norman and Amalie in July 1976, with his wife, Naomi, and two children, then ages eight and nine.

Naomi and Gerald Yablonsky offer this view of Norman and Amalie:

"Unless you knew what Norman and Amalie had been through in their youth, you wouldn't be able to tell on the surface that they had suffered so terribly," says Naomi, also a retired educator in the Newark schools. "They are warm and friendly neighbors. They had already been here a long time—since the neighborhood was built in the 1950s. We got to know them immediately when we moved in. I remember that their daughter was getting married that summer, and they talked about that with excitement."

As Jews, Gerald and Naomi are well informed about the Holocaust. Their families came to America nearly a century ago to escape anti-Semitism. Her ancestors came from Russia; his from the Ukraine and Russia. They have lived in New Jersey all of their lives and have had little firsthand experience with anti-Semitism. (A few rude comments, he says, over the years.) So, in some ways, the Holocaust is a foreign experience to them. Norman and Amalie have introduced them to this world and made them more conscious of it.

"I sometimes wonder how they do it," Naomi says. "I can only figure they must be extraordinarily strong people. I mean, to lose your loved ones brutally like that. To lose even *one* family member can destroy an entire family."

Do Norman and Amalie talk about it often? "If you ask, they will tell you what you want to know," she says. "Especially him."

"You can see that it is on their mind, especially his mind, all the time," Gerald adds. "One time he was out there shoveling snow, and I asked him if he should be doing that anymore. He's getting close to eighty, you know.

"His answer was, 'If I can work in the labor camps, I can shovel the snow in my own driveway.' And I said to him, 'Norman, you don't have to prove yourself anymore.'

"What I think I meant was, 'It's okay now; it's over.' But then I realized that for him, it is never over."

Chapter Seven

EMBRACING THE PAST

The day of my next visit arrives. This time I will talk to Amalie, but I have arrived just as she puts on a jacket and laces her walking shoes. It is time for her daily walk alone. She rarely misses it, even if the weather is bad. The doctor says it is good for her blood pressure.

But why go alone, without Norman? Is the daily walk for her health or perhaps her state of mind?

Amalie smiles. "I guess you could say it is for both," she says.

She needs a little break from Norman. The phone rings almost constantly; it is usually for Norman. It might be a scholar asking a question about the war or Jewish culture, or a teacher asking Norman to speak at a local school. Quite often it still involves business, for Norman, although officially retired as a builder and developer, has not been able to resist dabbling in his former career. Over Amalie's objections, he flew to Dallas recently to close a deal, the construction of a new apartment complex there.

"I think he is too old, too fragile to be traveling around like that by himself anymore," she says.

Norman does maintain a vigorous schedule, so much so that, unlike Amalie, he claims he does not have time to read the newspaper every day. Amalie, on the other hand, is a modern-age news junkie. She reads for hours every day, not just the local Jersey paper but a host of other publications, too. She is an avid reader of books on American history ("That's how I learned about my new country") as well as historical biographies. In the evening, she watches Dan Rather on CBS News, or the news on CNN.

The fact that Norman does not follow the news and contemporary culture as closely as she does is a regular source of friction.

"When did that happen?" Norman asks, overhearing us and clearly startled that he has somehow missed a story that has been making headlines. "How did I miss that?"

"If you read the newspaper every day, you wouldn't have to wonder," Amalie replies.

"Why didn't you tell me that happened? I feel like an idiot."

"What makes you think that's my job? What am I, a radio station? Read the newspaper yourself."

"I don't have time since I have so many important things to do."

"Like what?"

"Like all the bills! The letters!" he says, waving a handful of correspondence in the air to prove his point.

Amalie tosses her head like a debutante as if to say, "So what?" and abruptly leaves the house for her walk. From the window she appears as a chic suburban grandmother, the kind of woman you might see at an upscale shopping mall. She wears lipstick, even for a walk around the neighborhood. Her fashionable parka covers dark-colored leggings.

With Amalie out of the way, Norman decides this is a good time to give me a tour of the house, most specifically, it turns out, to show off his various collectibles. Amalie, he says, does not truly appreciate all of his treasures. In her view, they do little more than collect dust.

First, he wants to show me the basement, which, to my surprise, is crowded with piles of clothing, all neatly organized by size and category. Here is a box of shoes; over there, winter coats. It looks like a thrift shop.

"See, these are all things I send to Poland," he says proudly. "When I get a letter that someone needs something, I send it to them. Poland is a very poor country, you know, compared to the U.S."

Who are these people to whom he sends clothing, money, even medical supplies?

"Anyone who helped a Jew, any Jew, during the war," he said. "Christians who risked their lives for us. I can't stand the idea of them needing anything."

For years, he has collected clothing and supplies in good condition from family, friends, and neighbors. He packs the boxes and takes the bundles to be shipped from a port in New Jersey.

"My wife, in a way it drives her crazy because you can't even walk into the basement anymore," Norman says confidentially. "But she puts up with it because she agrees with what I am doing."

Then there are the boxes of correspondence relating to his latest project, begun in January 1998. In a unique fundraising effort, he is trying to raise six million pennies—one for each Holocaust victim—for the New York-based Jewish Foundation for the Righteous, which pays fourteen hundred monthly stipends to Christians or Muslims in twenty-six countries who rescued Jews during the war.

At this point, he has raised about $15,000 of his $60,000 goal, but he has already been successful in terms of spreading goodwill and calling attention to the organization. In parts of New Jersey, he is known as "the Penny Man" among schoolchildren, who often send small amounts to contribute to his campaign. One man sent him twenty-four thousand pennies that he had collected over forty years, and another, a check for $6,000.

Next stop on the tour is the garage. Norman, it seems, is a born collector. He can't, he says, resist browsing at flea markets and antique shops and often brings home a new treasure or two or three. Even in the garage, the walls are lined with automobile license plates, one for each year since Norman was born in 1920. Inside the house, each vase, tiny figurine, or miniature animal statue has a story: where he bought it, how much he paid for it, why he likes it, and so on. Talking about his treasures, perhaps, keeps his mind off the war years.

Upstairs, the closets of all four bedrooms are overflowing with Norman's books, photographs, and other memorabilia. Although much of it relates to the war years, there are signs that Norman's interests go far beyond. He has a particular interest in artwork and has collected information about the world's great painters. One wonders what Norman would have become if not for the war.

The closets are also the repository of Norman's extensive stamp collection, a hobby he began as a boy. As a child, he says, collecting stamps made him feel adventurous and connected to faraway places. The Germans took away his stamp collection, but after the war was over, he renewed his interest in philately as well as coins, even staying up all night on occasion to work on his new collections. His specialties are stamps and coins from Israel, Poland, the U.S., and to a lesser extent Germany and Russia.

One of the bedrooms is a guest room that seems to hold all of Norman's collectibles that simply won't fit in the living room. The furniture seems to have been pushed back each time a new trove of treasures arrives.

Another bedroom belongs to Esther, Norman and Amalie's

only child, who is now forty-two and lives in Boston. Although it has been more than two decades since Esther lived at home, Amalie and Norman leave her room largely unchanged. It is still "Esther's room." I can relate to this because although I am forty I, too, still have "my room" at my parents' house in New England.

The walls of the master bedroom are highlighted by large, cheerful photographs of Esther's three sons when each was a toddler. Like the rest of the house, the decorating has an elegant European flair.

It is the third bedroom that is unusual. Simply furnished with a single comfortable chair facing one wall, it is lined with carefully framed black-and-white photographs. Anyone sitting here cannot help staring at the photos, portraits of loved ones from another era.

Celia is here, smiling. So are David Petranker, Amalie's father, and her mother, Frieda. All of Norman's family is here, too. It is the emotional center of the house, even more so than the kitchen, the patio, or Norman's office.

Why here? Why not put the photos in the hallway or the living room?

Norman straightens them carefully, although they were not awry. He steps back, looking them over. For once, he has nothing to say.

Suddenly, it seems obvious that the placement of the family photographs honors the missing ones yet keeps their ever-present gaze separate from minute-by-minute existence in the house. Like a declaration or perhaps a truce, the choice to locate the photographs here seems to express Norman and Amalie's struggle to find a balance between embracing the past and yet keeping it, somehow, at bay.

When Amalie returns from her walk, she does not wish to discuss the room with the photographs. She says only that it is her favorite room for reading other than the kitchen, for the chair is comfortable, she explains, and the light is always good.

Nevertheless, we won't work in that room. Instead, she and I are back in the kitchen, sipping tea. She wants to tell me today about life with her father after the deaths of her mother and her sister Celia.

"We learned that the reason my mother and all the others were killed that day was that the Germans decided there were too many of us to fit in the ghetto where they wanted to confine us. It was inconvenient for them, so they reduced our numbers."

Amalie starts to say something else and falls silent. Suddenly, passionately, she adds, "I saw terrible, horrible things in the ghetto, but I also saw deeds of the greatest self-lessness and compassion among the Jews imprisoned there. The opposite, the very opposite of the behavior of the Germans. I saw mothers trying desperately to keep their children alive with soup that was mostly warm water with a few potato peels in it. I saw parents give the food from their mouths to their children. I saw children do the same for their parents. I saw strangers helping people on the street. Genia, the sister of one of my best friends, Betka Pipper, developed tuberculosis and refused to eat. She insisted that her share be eaten by her loved ones who had a better chance, she felt, at surviving."

I pause in my relentless note taking to marvel at the heroism of this young girl, Genia Pipper. Amalie reads my mind: "Yes, it was extraordinary," she says.

The weak and meek were the first to die—children, older people, the sick or fragile, Amalie says. It was not unusual to see people drop dead in the street from starvation. In the winter months, she saw many people who had simply frozen to death.

76

"To think that I was actually seeing such things with my eyes!" Amalie cries out. "Just a few months earlier I was a happy-go-lucky schoolgirl. My worries then were my grades at school and whether I'd get to go to the movies. I knew nothing about how to deal with this."

The Germans assigned ten Jews to a room, she recalls, and enforced the regulation fiercely. A growing number of Jews was forced into the ghetto every day, having been rounded up from different villages. At the same time, Amalie says, the Germans made less and less food available.

"Disgusting," I mutter under my breath.

"Diabolical," Amalie mutters under *her* breath.

Amalie and her father ended up staying at the home of a relative of Frieda's, a stepsister named Clara Hut, who happened to live in the ghetto limits. Amalie did not know her aunt Clara well; there had not been a close relationship between her and Frieda.

"But lucky me," she says with some amazement, "it turned out that this woman, my aunt Clara, treated me just like a daughter. I was surprised at how kind and tender she was with me; I hadn't expected it. And what a gift this was to me! Especially since I just lost my mother."

Also imprisoned within the ghetto was Amalie's boyfriend, Alek Lamensdorf. Alek's father, Stefan, had already died of starvation. Alek turned down opportunities to escape the ghetto because, Amalie tells me softly, he refused to leave behind his dying mother.

"He knew that he was resigning himself to death," Amalie says, bordering on tears. "The last time I saw him he looked like a skeleton, and I was very frightened for him. He said he couldn't bear the idea of letting his mother die alone. I tried to argue with him, but he was resolute. Before we said good-bye, he tried to give me something very precious, something that would have been worth a lot of money if he had sold it: the identity card of a Ukrainian Christian girl. I refused to accept it because I wanted him to sell it and use the money to buy food."

Amalie adds that she's happy that she didn't take it, for it was used by Alek's younger sister, Cesia, to board a train and leave Stanislawow. Alek had offered it to Amalie first because the ID card was much less likely to work for Cesia, who was far younger than the age of the Ukrainian Christian girl on the identity card. Somehow, it worked for Cesia anyway. She survived the war, harbored by a peasant family that was paid money by her uncle.

There were periodic *Aktionen* (raids) in the ghetto. Happily for Amalie and her father, they were issued Class A labor cards, which protected them somewhat because it meant they were healthy and able to work.

"The Germans had no use for people with Class B and Class C cards, who were mostly the old, the sick, and the disabled," Amalie says bitterly. "By the German way of thinking, anyone who was 'undesirable'—particularly Jews but also social outcasts like Gypsies, Jehovah's Witnesses, and homosexuals—was considered a burden and not worthy of living."

After a while, even having a Class A card was not much protection. It became increasingly clear that the Germans really intended to kill them all.

Amalie pauses for a moment, reflecting.

"What is it like," I ask tentatively, "to find out that you are considered *disposable*? That the dominant group has decided that you don't have any basic rights—not even the right to live?"

"It is probably not possible for you to understand fully because you are part of a majority," she says. "You are white, you are Christian, in America. You have to work hard to

78

come close to how we felt. What was it like? It was like we were less than human. Just imagine what it is like to be treated as if you are less than human."

Now Amalie leans forward, signaling that she has something especially important to say.

"During one *Aktion*, Aunt Clara, her husband, David, and my father and I were very nearly taken away," she says, "but the young Gestapo officer leading the raid recognized me."

It turned out that he was Willy Mauer, an officer who, she recalls with a shudder, seemed to take particular pleasure in harassing her back when she had been the maid for another Gestapo officer and his fiancée. Willy Mauer and his brother Hans burst into their apartment in the ghetto, and to her surprise, Willy seemed caught off guard by her presence.

"He must have felt some sort of human feelings toward me because he pushed me into a room and told me to stay there," Amalie says with bewilderment. "I saw my opportunity, and I begged him to let my father, my aunt and uncle be put in the room with me. Surprisingly, he relented, but not before beating my father with a rubber club."

The story gets worse. "When we looked out the window after they left, we witnessed Hans Mauer take out his gun and shoot a woman who was walking away from him," Amalie says, wiping away a tear that has crept into the corner of her eye. "Poor one, she tried to crawl away, but he fired two more shots, and she stopped moving. It was our former neighbor, Mrs. Richter, the woman who had witnessed what had happened to my mother in the cemetery."

As time went on, there were more *Aktionen*, and the Germans became increasingly savage. Some Jews were killed on the spot, literally in the street. Many Jews were sent off to "work" camps, never to be seen again. In actuality, they were sent to extermination camps.

Bizarre things continued to happen, including some moments of truly extraordinary good luck for a few individuals. Amalie tells me of the time the Germans went on a rampage in the streets and hanged one hundred Jewish men, members of a Jewish *Ordnungsdienst* selected by the Germans to help keep order in the ghetto.

"Listen to this," Amalie says. "The rope around the neck of one man broke, and he fell to the ground. Well, he got up and ran and just kept on running. Despite all the Germans there with their guns, somehow he got away. I know that he survived because I saw him again years after the war. He married and went on with his life. Today he is an old man, eighty-seven years old, living in Florida, playing golf—and I understand he plays a good game, too!"

Amalie chuckles, and so do I. It's a relief to have something to laugh about. But I need to wrap up the interview. We're nearly finished with this part, and I don't want to make Amalie come back to it another day. What, I ask, happened to Aunt Clara? And to your father?

Amalie looks pensive. She takes a sip of water, then speaks:

"One day, Aunt Clara and I were alone in the apartment when we heard the sounds of another raid—men shouting in German, screams, gunfire. Aunt Clara had this idea—I don't know why—that we should run and be with her daughter. For some reason, she thought we would be safer at the factory where her daughter was assigned to work. She begged me to come with her, but I refused, just as I had the day my mother was killed. Once again, my instincts turned out to be right. After Aunt Clara left our apartment, she was caught and taken along with many others to a death camp. She did not survive."

I am astounded by Amalie's intuition and say so.

80

"But you will laugh, darling, when you hear how I survived that day."

Well?

"I hid inside the baking oven. Yes, that's right. I climbed inside and stacked the wood in front of me! Obviously, the oven was cold, or I would not have been able to hide there. I squashed myself into a little ball and waited. Finally, I heard the door of the apartment burst open. I could hear men's heavy boots hitting the floors—oh, such a sound—as the Germans ran from room to room. After a while, I heard no more sounds. I waited as long as I dared and climbed out. It was a moment of triumph, for I had survived one more *Aktion*."

David Petranker, at work that day, was appalled when he learned later what had happened. Both father and daughter were weak and losing the "will to live." Increasingly desperate, David Petranker bribed an official to get himself and his daughter assigned to jobs at the railroad yard. His hope was that they might encounter some sympathetic Christians and perhaps some new avenues of escape, Amalie explains. They spent their days on hands and knees, scrubbing the railroad cars and the station floor, yet they still held on to hope.

About a month later, Amalie became sick with a fever. It was the first day of Rosh Hashana, the holiday when Jews celebrate the first day of the new year. Her father did not dare stay home to look after her, for failing to show up for work meant certain death.

"I locked myself in the apartment," Amalie recalls. "After a while I thought I heard voices yelling in German. *Was it real? Or was it from the fever? Was I delirious?*"

Unfortunately, it was indeed another *Aktion*. Hiding in the oven had worked once; maybe it would work again. Again, the German soldiers searched the apartment, and again, they did not discover her. But her happiness at fooling them was short-lived, for that night her father did not return home, she recalls.

Frantic, Amalie went to the railroad yard to search for him the next morning. An older woman approached her, perhaps trying to comfort her, and said she had overheard a Ukrainian policeman say that the men had been taken to a labor camp, most likely Maidanek.

"They'll be better off there than in the ghetto," she said. But Amalie knew that wasn't true. Maidanek, many of the ghetto residents already knew by then, was a death camp.

Amalie and her father had agreed earlier that if one of them disappeared or was taken away, the other should stay put for three weeks to wait for a sign or word from the other. If three weeks passed without any sign, the one left behind was to set out alone. Amalie worked for three weeks at the railroad yard, waiting and hoping, but there was no sign.

None ever came.

Amalie pauses, and I look up from my notes. I set my notes down on the table for a moment, letting her know that we can stop if she wants to. I wonder how she can speak at all. *It is no wonder*, I think, *that some Holocaust survivors took their own lives after the war*. It seems ironic to survive and then kill yourself, but looking into the pain deep within Amalie's dark-brown eyes, I can understand why someone might consider doing that.

"To make matters worse," Amalie is saying.

To make matters worse? What next? I grimace and immediately wish I hadn't. It seems rude. Stupid perhaps. So what if it's hard for me to hear this? I realize, instead, how hard it is for her to tell. I nod my head for her to continue.

"Near the end of the three weeks, I had slipped and cut my leg with an ax while chopping up an old piece of furniture for firewood. Silly, cosmopolitan girl that I was, I didn't even

82

know how to use an ax! This was a disaster because the Germans would kill anyone who was unable to work."

"Not to mention the fact," I interject, "that you had a nasty cut and couldn't go to a doctor for treatment."

Amalie nods her head. "This was true. I was in big trouble. The irony is that my injured leg led to my salvation. Because of it, I came to the attention of a young man named Mundek who had some authority at the railroad. He saw that I was injured, and he assigned me to 'work' in a rail car alongside him, where I rested and nursed the wound out of sight of the Germans."

"Mundek saved your life?" I ask.

She smiles. "Yes. He saved my life. He was my guardian angel. But I will tell you more about him another day."

Chapter Eight

A COUSIN'S STORY

The stately trees that line the streets of Englewood, New Jersey, have peaked in all nature's glory, their leaves covering the streets, lawns, and sidewalks on this fine autumn morning. Leaf blowers whine and men struggle with rakes, but a seventy-eight-year-old man trudges about in delight.

He is Leo Petranker, a first cousin of Amalie's, and I have come here, about an hour farther north of Norman and Amalie's house, to see what he might have to say. He has just returned from a stroll through his neighborhood to collect fallen leaves, the colors of which he wants to capture precisely in his next painting. Wearing a black beret and a striped sweater, he looks every bit the retired Manhattan art director that he is.

Leo Petranker's father, Oskar, and Amalie's father, David, were brothers. Leo's branch of the family lived in Germany during the time that Amalie was growing up in Poland. While he, too, is a Holocaust survivor, he speaks of Norman and Amalie's experiences with awe.

It has been six decades since Leo Petranker arrived in America, yet he is almost giddy about the privileges that Americans enjoy. "Walking down the street, anywhere you want! Incredible!" he says joyously. "Freedom of the press— amazing! This Monica Lewinsky mess—I love it! Everything in Nazi Germany was either black or white, *nein* or *ja* [no or yes]."

As a Jewish teenager living in Berlin during the rise of Hitler, Leo Petranker was a witness to the escalation of terror. He is acutely sensitive to the power of words.

"Always listen to the language of a people," he says. "When people use extreme words, like *assassinate*, this is a sign of trouble to come."

He remembers attending Adolf Hitler's public rallies and seeing him evolve from extremist to demigod. "Once, I was just a few feet from him, and the SS were all around him, but I saw women and men and children fall to their feet and kiss his boots," he recalls. "It was disgusting. They worshiped him! They were making a god from a human being."

A bright young man with boundless interests and energy, he studied under Martin Buber. Among his classmates was Albert Einstein. He saw Jesse Owens, the black American track star, make a fool of Hitler by winning at the 1936 Olympics.

He remembers *Kristallnacht*, the famous "night of broken glass," when the police stood by as Jewish shops, homes, and synagogues were destroyed. In fact, he says, he doesn't understand why *Kristallnacht* is frequently commemorated when there were so many nights "just as terrible."

In 1938, he escaped to Belgium, then to Holland, where he was considered an enemy alien because his nationality was German. From Holland he made it to England, then to Ireland, where they were "annoyed," he says, that he spoke English—eighty-seven words in all—with an English accent. At the end of 1938, he encountered his father, Oskar Petranker, in Ireland by "pure luck," and the two of them boarded a ship to America to join his mother and sisters, who escaped first and were waiting in Brooklyn. He was then seventeen years old.

How did he do it? How did he get from Berlin to New York?

"I was a vicious street fighter," he says matter-of-factly. "I was very agile, very fast, and I fought back brutally. It sounds horrible, but always hit 'em in the testicles. Works every time."

The minute he was eligible, in 1942, he became an American citizen. He immediately tried to enlist in the U.S. Army but was turned down because of ill health—the result of years of deprivation, such as eating sawdust, instead of flour, in bread. Desperate to do his part in the war effort, he volunteered at the State Department, where he translated a "massive amount" of material.

He married a young woman named Edith Mayer and settled into life in America, which, he says, is indisputably the best place in the world.

"In America, we have 187 nationalities all living together," he says, mentioning the figure off the top of his head. "It is incredible!"

Could the Holocaust happen here?

"No," he says, "I don't think so. I don't think the people would put up with it. The brilliance of America is the separation of church and state. It is an unbelievable achievement! Americans, learn from us Europeans! What you have accomplished is great, but you must protect it! And using one language—English—is very important! Bilingualism is a mistake; it divides people."

There is perhaps no greater patriot than Leo Petranker, who says with pride that he and Edith raised three children—Diane, Joyce, and Stephan, who are "totally, completely American."

What does he tell his grandchildren about the Holocaust?

"I tell them that it happened because the German people

were very disillusioned. There were economic causes, heavy unemployment. But I make it clear that there was already hatred, deep hatred. Protestants versus Catholics, and both of those groups versus Jews. This is what made the Holocaust possible."

He points out that in countries such as Denmark, citizens worked together to protect the Jews, and as a result, many survived.

"It's because of democracy!" he declares. "The places where democracy was strong is where the Jews survived. In a democracy, the majority understands that they must protect the rights of minorities."

What about Germany today? What about the young people?

He frowns. In 1991, he returned to Germany for the first time since the war to be a guest lecturer at several universities. "The students, I thought, seemed ignorant of the Holocaust," he says. "Maybe it's better now; I don't know."

Are Germans different from other people?

"Germans, even in a democracy, tend to be intolerant," he says. Suddenly, he smiles. "But it's not their fault they were born German, after all. What matters is that a person has *Menschlichkeit* [human compassion].

"If more people had intervened, or at least not aided the Germans as they did in Poland, many thousands of people could have been saved," he adds. "It is a miracle what Norman and Amalie went through, that they were able to live through all that."

During the war, he lost track of Amalie and her branch of the family. "We lost all communication with relatives in Poland," he recalls. "But we knew that as bad as things had been for us in Berlin, things must be worse for them. We knew about the destruction of Polish Jewry. I did not know Amalie's fate. I just assumed they were all dead."

Chapter Nine

AN UNSPEAKABLE EVENT

Going out to eat with Norman and Amalie is a fun affair, for they eat out regularly at several favorite area restaurants and they know the waitresses by name and the menus by heart. Since they do not "keep kosher," they eat wherever they want.

Today, we eat at a Greek diner, ordering the "special" and eating far too much food. Then we're back at the house, and it's Norman's turn to talk. We are in command headquarters (his home office). He has a lot more to tell me.

"I was very patriotic," he says wistfully. "When the Germans invaded Poland, my first impulse was to join the Polish army. I wanted to do my part, but I was turned down because I was a Jew. This was the first time I really understood that I was a *Polish Jew*. Before that, I had the idea that I was a *Pole* who was *Jewish*."

Having not lived through a war, I can only imagine the world I know under attack. It is very hard to picture.

Norman continues, "I'll tell you what it seemed like. It seemed like Poland was collapsing. The Germans seemed to be attacking everywhere, strafing and bombing in the farmland as well as the towns."

It was a week before the residents of Kolbuszowa were to see the arrival of a German tank, Norman recalls. The following day, there was a two-hour battle between the Polish army and the Germans. And then it was over.

"When we heard voices in the street yelling, *'Alle heraus!'* [Everyone out!], we found out who won," Norman says, grimacing at the memory.

As soon as the Jewish residents went out onto the streets, the Germans forced them to march to the edge of town, where they threatened to "burn us alive," Norman says. "Instead they left us there overnight, scared out of our wits. The next day they let us go home, except for two Jewish refugees from a nearby town who were hanged and five other Jews who were held hostage."

Almost immediately, many Jews were forced to become slave laborers. The healthiest young men, including Norman, then nineteen years old, were selected to do the things that the Germans would not do, Norman says, such as bury dead horses, clean up debris, and collect unexploded shells.

Beatings by the Germans occurred at whim and frequently. The first time Norman was beaten, he tells me, it was by a member of the SA, or Brownshirts, a man even younger than himself.

"I can still hear him screaming, *'Schneller, Jude, schneller, du Schweine!'* [Faster, Jew, faster, you pig!]," Norman says with a shudder.

Once, Norman was beaten because he was wearing nice clothes. "Don't show up for work wearing good clothes," was the explanation for the punishment. Then, Norman's best friend, Noah Hutner, was beaten for wearing *old* clothes to work.

Escape at that point was not difficult, though the price was death if you were caught, Norman recalls. One day, Norman and four of his friends simply set out for Russia, crossing at the San River, the new border between German and Russian troops.

"The Germans gave us no trouble because the policy at the

moment was to encourage Jews to cross over to Russia," Norman says, sounding almost amused. "Of course, we were then arrested by the Russians on the other side!"

The Russians were sending Jews to Siberia, so in the night the young men tricked their captors and escaped, walking farther into the Russian countryside. Norman, who had some distant relatives in Lvov, headed there. His relatives took him in without a moment's hesitation, he says.

"Now, this is going to sound strange to you," he says, apparently not realizing that all of this sounds strange to me. "But the next three months were among the happiest of my life! That's right! I enrolled in a school called Gymnasium Korkisa and became involved in the Gimpels Theater, a Jewish theatrical group. My first part was in the Yiddish play *In Polish Oyf der Keyt.*"

Norman had mentioned to me earlier that as a boy, he always thought he might become either a doctor or an actor, and I realize how much this opportunity must have meant to him.

Norman's other ambition was, naturally, to fight the Germans. Perhaps he might find a way to serve in the Russian army. But then it all changed, and he made a choice that would change his fate.

He got a message from his girlfriend, Rozia, back in Kolbuszowa. Rozia was alone with her mother, who was ill. Although Rozia did not ask him to return, he felt that was what he should do. In a matter of days, Norman recalls, he had slipped back across the border and made his way home to Kolbuszowa.

"Rozia was happy to see me, but very sad at the same time," he says. "My father was happy to see me, too, but immediately he said to me, 'Naftali, you have made a terrible mistake coming back here.' "

They were right. Soon Norman found himself forced to be a slave laborer again; he became an inmate at two different camps. One was the prison camp at Lipie, a village in the Carpathian Mountains, where he spent his days breaking up rocks and moving debris from one place to another. The other was the Pustkow concentration camp, which was southwest of Kolbuszowa. At Pustkow, among the incentives to make the inmates behave, Norman reports, was a "twice-daily ritual in which innocent men were hanged before our eyes."

Norman shakes his head in disgust. Suddenly, he brightens. "I must tell you about one of my heroes from this era. He was a man who made this time more tolerable for many, many people, and he deserves to be remembered. His name was Dr. Leon Anderman. Before the war, he was not at all involved in the Jewish community, but after the war started, he became very involved. He became our leader. I got to know him well because he taught me to help him run an *ambulatorium* he set up for our sick and wounded. He taught me how to dress wounds and do minor procedures."

Norman recalls that when the order came to wear armbands bearing the Star of David, Dr. Anderman was the first to put on his armband, and he walked "through the town with his head held high, making a point of showing that he was proud." That was not what the Germans had in mind. They called the armbands *die Schande Bande*, the sign of shame, according to Norman. Eventually, Dr. Anderman was sent to Auschwitz concentration camp. He never returned. Clearly, the whole community suffered a great loss.

Like Amalie's family, Norman's family members were forced to move into a ghetto in their town, and they began to see that what was happening to them was part of a larger pattern. The Germans, quite simply, wanted to create a world that was *Judenrein* (without Jews). Jews from small towns were sent to bigger towns, then forced into ghettos where they starved or died of disease.

"Why," I ask, "were you put in ghettos?" This part has always confused me.

Norman frowns. "To make it easy for the Germans to send large numbers of us to the extermination camps."

"Did you ever really expect such a thing could happen? That they wanted to kill all of you?" The words do not roll off my tongue easily.

Norman nods. "Well, no one in the history of the world had ever tried such a thing. It is part of being human to have hope, especially when there is no—what is the word?— precedent for what is happening to you. For this reason, we still had some hope."

I want to hear more about the Kolbuszowa ghetto. Norman has no difficulty recalling every detail. "Basically, it was a sealed area that included the old synagogue and a few other Jewish institutions." He describes a heartbreaking scene of the Jewish people struggling with their few possessions as they were relocated to the Kolbuszowa ghetto.

"I can see them now: Naftali Nessel and his sons lugging a stand for splitting logs. There was Basheh the baker, who dragged behind her the boards she used for making bagels. There was my old schoolteacher, struggling to carry his school bench."

The Kolbuszowa Jews were relocated again later to the ghetto in Rzeszow. After a few weeks, the Saleschutz family was among many who were able to return to Kolbuszowa by paying a substantial bribe. At that time the entire extended family was able to live at Leibush's house, which fortunately was within the ghetto limits. Norman explains that his parents' home, along with all of the others in the marketplace, had already been declared the property of the German government.

It was at Leibush's house that the Saleschutzes would have their last Sabbath dinner together as a family. It was June of 1942, three years after the war started in Poland. "Strangely enough, despite our situation and everything going on around us, we were happy that night—just happy to still be together," Norman recalls with a sad smile. "It was the most touching Sabbath dinner of my entire life."

Not long after, events took a sharp turn for the worse. There was a sudden pounding at the door one day. Knowing the Germans were very likely coming for the men of the family, two of the five sisters and their mother bolted the door while their father and brothers rushed out the back.

This is how Norman describes that day, his voice tense and rising:

"Leibush and I raced across our yard to a neighbor's house. We hid in the attic. My sister Matl took my father to an outhouse in our yard and locked him inside with a padlock. She was hoping to make it appear that no one was inside.

"But Matl must have decided he was not safe there. A few minutes later, she went back. Just as she was unlocking the padlock, a Gestapo officer saw her and told her to stop. A second Gestapo officer came into the yard dragging Israel Hofert, our neighbor, and forced him to identify my father. My father's name was on the list of those they were looking for that day. Both Gestapo officers drew their guns and started to push my father into a shed that we used to keep firewood.

"From a small window in the attic where Leibush and I were hidden, I could see Matl, who was screaming. She stepped between my father and the Gestapo officers. Then

Rachel came running outside and begged them not to hurt our father. They hit both of my sisters, knocking them to the ground. Then they pushed my father into the shed and out of my view.

"I heard the sound of two gunshots. A moment later I heard my father's voice. He was wounded but still alive. I heard him yell, 'Pigs! Executioners!' and then *'Nekuma! Nekuma! Nemt Nekuma!'* [Revenge! Revenge! Take revenge!].

"In his last moments, my father called out the prayer of the Jew: *'Shema, Yisrael, Adonai Elohenu, Adonai Echod'* [Hear, O Israel, the Lord is our God, the Lord is One].

"The Gestapo officers had left, but upon hearing my father's defiant screams, they returned. There were five more shots. Then it was quiet."

For the first time in all my conversations with Norman, he appears grief-stricken. He is unable to continue for a few minutes. He leans his face into his hands.

"The worst part is, I feel the guilt," he says, his voice strained and faraway. "I felt humiliated that this happened and I had witnessed it, ashamed that I was not able to help, that I didn't even try."

"What happened next?" I ask gently.

"I ran from my hiding place and across the yard. Maybe the Germans were somewhere nearby, but I didn't care. I saw my father's body, covered with blood, with my mother and my sisters kneeling around him weeping."

Just then, Norman recalls, a third Gestapo officer arrived on the scene. Somewhat surprisingly, he did not shoot Norman. Instead, he told Norman and a Jewish "policeman"—a sixteen-year-old boy named Itchele Silber—to bury the men killed in the *Aktion* that day at the Jewish cemetery.

"I knew all of the men I had to bury, all twenty-two of them," Norman says. "In some cases, the bodies were still warm, if you can imagine such a thing. The worst was to bury my own father. I leaned on a tree at the cemetery, sobbing and hitting the tree with my fists."

As an act of respect for his father, and an act of rebellion against the Germans, Norman enlisted Leibush's help in finding a way to keep their father from being buried in a common grave with the others. Norman put his father's body in the cart with his feet sticking out. "As we went past our grandfather's grave, Leibush and I pulled out the body," he recalls. "We covered him with brush, with branches.

"The next day I returned to rebury my father's body properly," Norman recalls grimly. He was laid to rest "next to my grandfather, which is what my father expected his whole life. That's the least I could do for him."

The others were reburied properly, too. "Each one, including my father, was buried with a knife in his hand, which signifies revenge. It indicates that they were murdered. This is a very old tradition."

That night, the Saleschutz family lit a candle, a Jewish tradition when someone has died, Norman says. "It was very ironic," he adds quietly. "We could not get candles during the war so easily, and my father had been saving little scraps and preparing a candle to mark the anniversary of his own father's death, which was in a few days.

"Instead, we used it to mark his."

Chapter Ten

A GUARDIAN ANGEL

To someone who escaped the Holocaust, food has a special significance, Amalie is explaining to me. Two weeks have passed since my last visit. We are back in the kitchen, she in "her" chair and I in "mine."

"You see, when you have been half-starved, you appreciate—really appreciate—food for the rest of your life," Amalie is saying to me as she examines a bowl of fruit on the table to see what is ripe. "Especially fresh fruits and vegetables, things that we could only dream about during the war. Vitamins. Nutrients."

She says the words respectfully, as if they are sacred. I, on the other hand, just eat without thinking much about it. Or do I? No, now I see food through their eyes. A beautiful strawberry is a work of art; a fine piece of salmon is a precious gift to be savored. Never again will I take food for granted.

"Now, where were we?" Amalie asks rhetorically. "Ah, yes, I was telling you about my guardian angel, Mundek." We settle into our chairs.

"Mundek's real name was Edmund Abrahamovitch, which he changed to Edmund Sultanski after the war," Amalie says, pausing to spell it for me. "He was from a tiny sect known as Karaites who lived in two towns, Halitz and Troki."

I draw a blank. "What, or who, are Karaites?" Amalie and Norman have been enormously patient with me. I know that at times I must seem ignorant to them, yet they have never made me feel bad about it.

"The Karaites were a sect that had split off long ago from mainstream Rabbinic Judaism," Amalie explains. "You see, the German authorities in Mundek's town, Halitz, had decreed that the Karaites were Turks, not Jews, and were to be left alone."

This quirk of fate meant that Mundek was a free man. But his sympathies were clearly with the Jewish people. Amalie would learn later that Mundek had helped eleven other Jewish girls, but she was the only one to survive the war.

The others did not survive, she says, because "they were Aryan looking and worked in Polish enterprises. And they would date the boys there. When the boys would get fresh with them, the girls refused their advances, and the boys would say something like, 'You act like a Jewess.' And unfortunately, the fear in their eyes gave them away. It was the fact that they could not disguise their feelings that did them in. One thing led to another, and they were turned in to the Germans.

"I owe my survival," she adds, "to the fact that God gave me such happy, shining eyes—Jews were said to have 'sad' eyes—and the ability to hide my feelings. Most people, like the other girls Mundek tried to help, when they feel fear, it shows in their eyes, but this was not true for me."

Mundek hid Amalie temporarily at his mother's home in Halitz and then helped her to get new identity papers.

"My identification card indicated that I was a Jew. Obviously, this was not good. So Mundek talked to a Polish friend who worked for a scrap metal company who agreed to provide papers that indicated I was an employee there," Amalie explains. "I remember the day Mundek asked me, 'What name do you want to use?' It was such a strange moment! Imagine, I had to select a new identity!"

She says she chose Felicia, because it means "good luck" in Latin, and Milaszewska, because it was the name of her favorite Polish female author. She kept her birth date—October 21, 1922—the same so that there was "one less thing to remember" in case she was interrogated.

"And so that is how Amalie Petranker, a Jewish schoolgirl, became Felicia Milaszewska, a Polish Gentile girl," Amalie says with a big smile. "Imagine that. It sounds like something out of the movies."

Amalie's demeanor quickly changes, however, as she moves on to the next story she will tell me today. "This is going to be very hard for me, but I must tell you what happened to my father."

A month went by, she recalls, before she learned his fate. Mundek was the one who found out, but he could not bring himself to tell her right away. This is what she learned from Mundek and was later confirmed by witnesses:

"My father had been put on a cattle car transporting Jews to Belzec, a death camp," she says. "With his bare hands, my father tore up two floor boards. He asked if anyone would jump with him, but they were too afraid, except for one teenage girl. My father and this girl, they dropped between the wheels of the moving train! They were badly bruised and scraped up, but they managed to walk to a nearby peasant's home. My father told the peasant woman that he was looking for work. Apparently, he acted as if this girl was his daughter. The peasant woman's husband was being held as a prisoner in Russia, so she asked no questions. She needed workers.

"This is the part that kills me, that hurts me so," Amalie says, her voice rising. "My father was only one hour's walk from where I was hidden by Mundek. We were just a short distance from one another and never knew it. We were both safe," she repeats, "and we never even knew it."

David Petranker, believing Amalie was still in the ghetto in Stanislawow, left the peasant's house and headed back to find her. It was a bold and fateful decision. To board a train, for a Jew, was almost certain death because the trains were heavily patrolled. He knew the risk, his daughter says tearfully these many years later. But he went anyway.

"Maybe he was like Alek with his mother; he just couldn't live with himself if he had left you behind," I say, searching for words to comfort her.

"It's my fault," she says. "Everyone tells me it's not my fault; I shouldn't feel that way."

"I would blame myself, too."

"You would?"

"Absolutely."

"Even though you knew, factually, that it wasn't your fault? That it was his choice to go on the train?"

"Definitely. Of course."

Amalie seems to like my answer. She does not need people to persuade her to feel differently from the way she does. I wait for her to continue her story.

"Once on the train, my father was recognized by a former friend and business associate, a Ukrainian man. Mundek learned that this man left his seat and located the German railroad police and pointed out my father."

Amalie cannot understand why this man did not simply look the other way. "He didn't have to turn him in. They knew each other. Why did he do it? Why?"

David Petranker was taken to a location known as Rudolf's Mill in Stanislawow and executed there.

"And so I became an orphan. Not only that, but I had to live with the fact that my father, my poor, dear father, had sacrificed his life for mine."

Amalie was nineteen years old. Her only hope was that if she could survive the war, and the Allies won, at least she had Pepka and a few other relatives in Palestine—three uncles (her mother's brothers) and a grandmother, Rifka Genger (her mother's mother).

"At this time," Amalie says weakly, "I began to wonder if maybe God was keeping me alive for a reason. *Perhaps*, I thought, *he wanted me to bear witness, to tell the world what happened. Maybe staying alive would be the only way, in a sense, to defeat the Germans.*"

But there was not much time to contemplate such things. Amalie soon realized, she says, that she was a burden on Mundek's mother who, after all, was at great risk for hiding Amalie. Uncomfortable with the situation, Amalie persuaded Mundek to take her to Lvov, the nearest large city to Halitz, during the winter of 1942–43.

"It did not go well for me in Lvov," Amalie says simply. "Mundek had this idea that he would keep me hidden at the apartment of his cousin, but the cousin frightened me. He was lecherous and crude, and you know I had been sheltered from such things and couldn't cope with it. I left there immediately and found a place to stay at a boardinghouse, but this was extremely dangerous. The very first night there was a raid, and I was very nearly taken away."

The rumor on the streets was that the best place for a Jew to pass as a Christian was in Cracow. Many Jews throughout Europe were trying to "pass," and only the tiniest fraction were able to fool the Germans, but Amalie felt it was her only option. She thanked Mundek for all that he had done, but told him it was time she set out on her own, risks and all.

Nothing—not a single step—was easy, Amalie recalls. "Getting to Cracow was easier said than done. It meant taking the train south to Stryj and then transferring to a different train that headed west to Cracow. The train stations were swarming with Germans. All I had for identification was a little slip of paper stating my new name and that I worked for a certain scrap iron company!"

She had no family in Cracow, but remembered that her father's boss, a Christian named Kazimir Jerzenicki, had fled to Cracow with his family when the Russians came to Stanislawow in 1939.

"Luckily for me, he was listed in the phone book," Amalie remembers. "I went to his home and knocked on the door. It was a stylish part of town. His wife, a kind and lovely woman, answered the door and let me in. Here I stayed for three weeks, masquerading as the family's new governess."

But they were a Polish family with many Polish servants, and she remained in great danger. "Worse, to me, was that I was putting my benefactors in jeopardy," Amalie says. "I could not have lived with myself if one of the servants had learned I was a Jew and gone to the police. It would have meant the end not only for me but for Mr. and Mrs. Jerzenicki and their beautiful young children."

Amalie reflects on this for a moment. "Death was the price one paid for helping a Jew! I can understand why so few Gentiles helped us since the price was death if they were caught. But what I can't forgive are those who *went out of their way to turn us in*—like the man on the train who turned in my father."

Amalie concluded that the safest place might be "right in the midst of the lions' den." And so, with Mrs. Jerzenicki's help, Amalie got a job as the live-in maid and governess for the three children of a German official.

"Little did they know they were harboring a Jew," Amalie says, laughing. "They were thrilled to find a Polish girl who spoke fluent German. They seemed like a normal family like any other, and it was hard to believe that this was the enemy who was intent on exterminating my people."

On one level, she says, she hated them. Yet she needed them to survive. At any rate, she was not there long, for she suddenly became ill when a frightening abscess developed on her neck. There was no choice but to have it removed surgically.

"To go in a hospital, you needed papers," Amalie says. "This was a terrifying development."

Fortunately, her German employer made the arrangements, "getting me into the finest hospital, with the best doctors," Amalie says with an ironic smile. "The name of it was Saint Lazar Hospital."

While she was hospitalized, she feared she would say something that would reveal her identity, especially while under anesthesia. But she saw a nurse whom she suspected might be Jewish and begged her for help. "She did not admit to being Jewish," Amalie says, "but she watched over me. She even cleaned up my leg where I cut it with the ax. It was oozing and infected."

Also while she was in the hospital, Amalie befriended a girl in the same ward whose name was Kazia. She was a Polish girl, a Christian, who worked as a maid in a German club in Cracow. The club was operated by the Carpathian Oil Company for its German employees.

Kazia mentioned to Amalie that it was a pleasant place to

work, and after becoming friendly with her, Amalie asked if she could perhaps get a job there, too, Amalie recalls. Kazia, thankfully, was only too happy to help.

"And so I began my new career as a chambermaid," Amalie says, smiling, "which, frankly, I found much more tolerable than caring for the German official's children."

She made friends with the other girls, worked diligently, and kept her secret. She hoped to finish out the war there.

"When the Germans suffered defeat at Stalingrad," she says gleefully, "I was thrilled. I secretly rejoiced."

But she had discovered that two other girls working at the club also were Jews posing as Christians. One of them, a girl named Katia, had been quite hostile to Amalie. "Their feeling was that it was too dangerous for several Jews to try to masquerade in one place," Amalie recalls. "Since I came last, they thought I should leave. I promised to leave as soon as I could get better documents."

Katia was a medical student, a little older than Amalie. She was masquerading as a Ukrainian, Amalie recalls. "We met while I was in the hospital. Kazia had introduced us and was mystified that Katia reacted so coldly to me. But Katia had recognized that I was a Jew.

"Eventually, I was able to talk to Katia, and it was an enormous help to me to have someone to confide in," Amalie recalls, "though, of course, we had to be incredibly careful not to be overheard."

Katia helped Amalie out of an especially bad predicament. The club expected its workers to take a one-week, annual vacation with their families. Amalie had nowhere to go, but did not want to arouse suspicion.

She went to Katia for advice. Katia had left the club to become the housekeeper for a female German doctor. The doctor was leaving to go away for a month, and Katia offered to let Amalie stay there.

"It turned out to be one of the best weeks for me during the entire war years," Amalie says, "for I was able to relax. It meant so much to have a break from it all, to be normal. I could be Amalie again, not Felicia, and talk freely to someone who understood my situation. I could let my guard down. We questioned whether we would ever be normal again, would we ever be able to laugh again? I believe these conversations gave me new energy to keep going."

Later, back at the club, things seemed to be going smoothly. Amalie thought she was doing a pretty good job masquerading as Felicia. Then, she says, she learned just how vulnerable she really was.

"I was not fooling everyone. They had switched me to waitressing from being a chambermaid. I was not especially good at either! Then one day, a handsome German businessman named Jurgen asked me to come up to his room," Amalie tells me. "This was a respectable club, and naturally, I was offended, but he let me know that there was something important he had to tell me. With great reluctance, I went to his room. He asked me if I wanted something to drink, and I declined. I turned to walk out, and he said, 'I didn't think you would want a drink. Generally speaking, Jews aren't fond of drinking.' "

Amalie says she tried to act nonchalant. "I wouldn't know, really."

He walked across the room toward her while she stood there, unsure what to do next. "He had something to show me: a picture of an old, bearded Jew. 'It's my grandfather,' he said. 'My grandfather was a Jew.' " He went on to say that she was not safe at the club, that since he had figured out she was Jewish, someone else would, too. What had given her away? She didn't look like the other waitresses, who were

104

Polish peasant girls. It wasn't so much her features, but her manner, which was, Jurgen thought, too sophisticated.

"I have a very good friend at the railway authority," he told her. "A recommendation from me would mean a good job at one of the construction companies."

Amalie recalls that her head was spinning. To trust, or not to trust? She decided to see how things developed. Sure enough, within days, she received a job offer from Herr Langert, the German owner of a construction firm.

The construction company had two offices, a main office in Zwickau in Saxony (Germany) and a second one in Prokocim, a suburb of Cracow. It was at Prokocim that Amalie began her work as a secretary—and where Jewish inmates from the concentration camp at Plashow were "employed" as slave laborers.

"At one point I found a way to visit the field office with the naïve intention of helping my fellow Jews," Amalie recalls. "Oh! Sometimes I was so naïve! It very nearly backfired on me because one of the Jews there mentioned offhandedly that I looked 'just like' his niece. Well, the last thing I needed was a Jewish man, in front of my German boss, pointing out that I looked like a Jewish girl!"

What did she do? "I laughed it off, saying, 'Is your niece very pretty?' as if it was all a big joke, and it worked."

Back at the main office, she had many close calls but always managed to land on her feet. One of the worst incidents occurred when a Gestapo officer named Mueller—"a notorious killer and torturer from the concentration camp at Plashow," Amalie says—arrived at the office with two German shepherd dogs.

Mueller noticed that Amalie could not take her eyes off the dogs.

"He said to me, grinning, 'Don't be afraid of them. They

are trained to attack Jews only. In fact, they can smell one out a mile away.'

"I wanted to die right there, but I replied calmly, 'They must be very intelligent.'"

Then Mueller actually asked her for a date! "Are you free on Sunday evening?" he asked. She told him, "I'm sorry, but I have a boyfriend."

There were other bizarre moments. One day in the late fall of 1943, Amalie received an invitation from the director of the Deutsche Reichsbahn (German Railroad Authority) to attend a party as his escort at the headquarters of the Railroad Authority.

"Oh, what a needless risk this was!" Amalie recalls. "However, I couldn't refuse the invitation without arousing suspicion. I tried to get out of it. I told him, 'I am Polish, and I understand that only Germans are allowed to attend.'"

"Nonsense!" he replied. "You speak German well, and no one has to know you are a Pole."

And so she went, "little Amalie Petranker, the Jewess, posing as Felicia Milaszewska, the young Polish woman—who tonight was posing as a German!"

It was a surreal evening. All around her were beautiful, well-dressed women and their men, clicking their heels and giving the Nazi salute. She says she had to fight the urge to become physically sick. Among those present, she recalls, was a high government official. She tried to avoid him, but her escort insisted she meet him, introducing her as a "Baltic German."

This is how she describes what happened:

"He smiled at me charmingly and remarked at the rose on my lapel, that it was a *pulchra rosa* [Latin for pretty rose].

106

"Only *pulchra*? Why not *pulcherissima* [very beautiful]?" I asked coyly.

"Oh, you know Latin?" he said. "I salute you." Raising his glass, he announced to the entire room, "May all the German girls be as well educated as this little Baltic German."

The exquisite irony of this situation is not lost on Amalie, who says she still wonders how she kept her mouth shut.

"There was a part of me that wanted to scream, 'I am a Jew, you fools, you murderers!' It might have been worth dying at that moment just to see the looks on their faces. But there was another part of me that said, 'Live, despite all their best efforts to deny you life! Live, and be witness to what has happened to the Jews of Europe!'"

During the summer of 1944, even though there was new hope that the war would end soon, Amalie began to question whether she could hold on much longer. The Allies had invaded France, and the Russians were steadily pushing closer to Cracow. Perhaps the Jews would be saved—if there were any left. But as the Germans began to retreat, they did not abandon their efforts to exterminate the Jews. In fact, they actually redoubled their efforts.

One day, Amalie took an enormous risk. The office where she worked was located on a hill overlooking the Prokocim railroad station, a waystop on the death trip to Auschwitz. On that particular day, a transport of Czech Jews was stopped at Prokocim while Amalie was talking to a company engineer, a young Polish man.

"Suddenly, we could hear the sounds of thousands crying for help, for water," Amalie says, still anguished these many years later. "That man, his response was to smile sarcastically. I completely lost my mind for a moment, I was so full of rage. I didn't care what happened to me. I filled a pail of water and took it to the cattle cars. I gave water to the people trapped inside until a Ukrainian policeman thrust a gun into me, into my ribs. He took the pail of water and poured it on the ground. 'Beat it or I'll shoot you!' he screamed."

Her small act of rebellion nearly cost her life, but it was worth it, Amalie says. "There were some moments when I really did not care if I lived or died, and this was one of them."

Chapter Eleven

A LAST LETTER
FROM MOTHER

The weather now is much colder outside. The heat is on, and the air inside the cream-colored house is toasty.

Today Norman has asked me to help him write a letter. His spoken English is better than his writing, he says, and he doesn't want to make a fool of himself. Amalie's English is better than his since she studied it formally in school back in Poland.

With me around, Norman has a new person to ask for help. The letter he wishes to write today is a letter to the editor of a Jewish newspaper. Norman cannot resist speaking out on any issue related to the Holocaust. And the more agitated he is, the worse his English becomes, he says.

After I edit the letter for him, we turn to our discussion for the day. He wants to pick up where we left off last time. He forgot to tell me what happened that day to the old rabbi of Kolbuszowa.

"The rabbi, he was on the same death list as my father, but his family managed to hide him that day," Norman says. "He was totally blind and helpless, dependent on somebody to take him by the arm and lead him. I was asked to help smuggle him out of the ghetto. We cut off his beard, dressed him like a peasant, and took him, the back way, to a bench by the roadside where he was supposed to be picked up by his family."

Norman recalls a moment of despair. "I wasn't sure I saw the use in trying. I couldn't imagine what good this would do, to help get the old rabbi out of the ghetto. *Surely*, I thought, *he will be caught and killed, if not now, then later*. And that is what happened just two weeks later. His two granddaughters, Malka, eighteen, and Rachel, sixteen, begged the SS officer not to shoot him. He was shot anyway, along with the two girls."

The thought of these two teenage girls trying to protect their blind grandfather is almost more than I can bear. Especially since they were then killed, too. I glance out the window. What am I doing here? I want to run away. I want to go outside and walk in fresh air.

"You know, there were a lot of heroes like those girls," Norman says. "You just don't hear about it because the heroes usually died.

"The only good thing to say about the Holocaust," he adds, "is that at least the Jews did what we could to help each other. There was, of course, a sense that you had to look out for yourself, and naturally, there were some Jews who put their own survival ahead of everyone else. But for every one Jew who did that, there were a thousand or more who risked themselves to help family, friends, even strangers. I can promise you that."

It reminds me of an incident, apparently not uncommon, that I read about at the Holocaust Memorial Museum library in Washington. Jews forced to work at the death camps occasionally recognized their own family members among those assigned to death. When that happened, the workers would sometimes simply stop what they were doing and go to their deaths with their family members, forsaking any chance of survival.

Norman nods when I repeat this story. "Yes, I have heard

this many times." His own family, he points out, often took risks to help each other.

"Let me tell you a story," he says. "Shortly before my father was murdered, I became very ill, and my sisters Gela and Rechla, along with my brother Leibush, took an enormous risk for me. I had been sick with what was probably dysentery. Just as I began to feel better, I suddenly developed a horrible pain deep inside my ear.

"By the time we were able to locate a doctor, I was told I had a middle ear infection that had reached the lining of my brain. There was no choice; we had to get to Cracow because there was a Jewish hospital there. Through bribes, we managed to get on a train. The train ride was like a scene from hell. We were threatened, and another Jewish passenger was thrown off from the moving train by an angry mob of Poles.

"Convinced that we would be killed if we stayed on the train, we got off halfway to Cracow in the town of Tarnow. Thankfully, we had a cousin living there. As it turned out, there was still a Jewish hospital in Tarnow after all. On staff was a famous doctor. His name was Dr. David Rabinowicz, and he was formerly chief surgeon at one of the largest hospitals in Lodz. His nickname was Golden Hands.

"My sisters took me to see him. He said he needed to operate immediately. I overheard him say, 'This boy is 90 percent in the next world.'" He told my sisters that if I lived, I would be paralyzed, blind, deaf, or feeble-minded.

"Well, I survived the surgery with no problems at all— none. When the time came to say good-bye to Dr. Rabinowicz, I told him if he ran into problems in Tarnow, he should come to us in Kolbuszowa, where he would be treated like family. When I said this to him, his eyes filled with tears."

"Norman," I interrupt, amazed. "You really do have nine lives."

"Yes, but Dr. Rabinowicz did not."

"What happened to him?"

"He was killed."

"What?"

"He was dragged outside the hospital and shot dead in the yard one day. He had performed emergency surgery on a Polish man. It was illegal for a Jewish doctor to do that, and so the Germans murdered him. They killed a man for helping another! They killed a doctor for saving a life! And from the world, they stole a brilliant surgeon!"

We both sit in silence for a while, depressed. Norman finally clears his throat and speaks.

"Do you know what is ironic? That once I got back to Kolbuszowa, my life had just been saved, but I was in danger of being killed at any moment." Life in Kolbuszowa, at that time, was in the control of Herr Landskommissar Walter Twardon, a half-German and half-Polish man who announced, when he arrived, that Jewish life meant nothing to him, according to Norman.

"Twardon quickly became the chief executioner in our town," Norman continues. "A week before Passover in 1942, I saw him shoot and kill Itchele Trompeter, a very well-liked young man in our town who had just gotten married. Itchele was killed on the spot for trying to smuggle a pound of butter!"

Again, silence. I can't think of anything to say that wouldn't sound stupid in this context. And Norman seems lost in his thoughts.

"I will tell you this," Norman finally says. "That night, I remember it seemed like the whole town was crying."

Norman explains that the Germans tried constantly to extort money and luxury items from the Jews. The Jews hid pocket watches, trinkets, or anything of value to use for bribes when they needed something. Everyone, except the very poorest, found ways to hide things to barter for their survival, Norman says.

Under Twardon, this practice increased greatly. The German policemen would present the *Judenrat* with a list of things that the Germans "required." Jews would be killed if the items were not presented in a certain period of time, Norman recalls.

Meanwhile, they were forced to resettle in the ghetto in Rzeszow for a second time.

"We didn't know it at the time, but this was to be the last stop on the way to the death camps," Norman says quietly. "As soon as we got there, Twardon announced he was looking for a hundred able-bodied men to return to Kolbuszowa to demolish the Jewish ghetto. Leibush and I talked it over and decided to volunteer, thinking we might be able to use our contacts back home to get food for our family."

And so they left, Leibush and Norman, to go back home. Their job turned out to be a sadistic assignment, to tear down the buildings of the Jewish community that they so dearly loved.

"You can't imagine how sickening this was," Norman says with disgust. "With each board we tore from a building, we were destroying centuries of Jewish life. It was worse than the death of a person; it was the death of an entire way of life, of a culture. This is where we were born, lived, and died. And they were making us wipe it off the face of the earth as if it—we—never existed."

Knowing Norman as I now do, I know that he must have found some way, short of losing his life, to rebel.

"Yes, this is true," he says, and his eyes twinkle with mischief. "We were supposed to destroy everything, but whenever I came across photographs from somebody's family album, I took them. Whenever I had the chance, I hid these photos in barns all over the countryside. First, I wrapped them to protect them from the weather. I am very proud to say that these photographs survived the war. In most cases, it is all that is left of the people to show that they lived."

Photography has always been one of Norman's special interests. When he was a boy, he recalls begging his brother in America to bring him a camera when he came to Poland. That is how Norman got his first camera, an old Brownie.

"I didn't know it at the time, but I was documenting many people and places that would be lost forever," he tells me. Yet the worst was to come.

While Leibush and Norman labored in Kolbuszowa, the rest of the family was taken away. His mother sent a letter that she wrote just before it happened.

She wrote, "I don't know what will become of us. We will, it seems, share the fate of the whole community. But you, Naftali, are young and strong, and your duty is to live. Don't let orphanhood break your spirit. Stay alive, and when the war is over, let the world know what the Germans did, what kind of murderers they are!"

When Leibush and Norman found out that the rest of the family had been taken away, they were almost paralyzed with grief and fear, Norman recalls. But they realized they would have to act immediately if there was any hope of finding and rescuing them. They hired a local Polish man to investigate their loved ones' whereabouts, but the news he brought back was anything but good.

Norman tells it this way:

"They were taken to Belzec, the death camp. My married sisters and their husbands and children, along with my girlfriend, Rozia, were taken on July 7. My mother, my two unmarried sisters, and Leibush's wife and three children

114

were taken on July 17. All had been killed, gassed, and burned at Belzec."

Except for their older brothers—Al in America and David in Palestine—there were just the two of them left, Leibush and Norman.

"Without even discussing it, we knew we would stick together," Norman says softly. "I was all he had, and he was all I had. Besides, I didn't think Leibush could survive without me. For one thing, he looked less Slavic and more Jewish than I did. And another thing—Leibush did not speak very good Polish, and I spoke it fluently. So Leibush, who was sixteen years older than me, and had just lost his wife and three children as well as our mother and sisters, was dependent on me."

Leibush, however, had one major advantage over everyone else: he was unusually strong and powerful, Norman says. In fact, the Germans could not get over how strong he was and often made him demonstrate his strength. Leibush was intelligent but had little formal education. He had grown up during World War I, and like many of his peers, his education had been disrupted.

Leibush and Norman continued to work at the Kolbuszowa Labor Camp, as it was called, under Twardon. For reasons Norman didn't understand at the time, Twardon liked him. Years later, he says, he read in a book published in Poland that Twardon had been a homosexual.

"He had this idea I was some kind of ladies' man, which wasn't true," he says, "but I let him believe it and used it to my advantage."

How?

"Once, I was stopped, and I had some walnuts with me, a real luxury. They would kill a Jew for having such a thing. I convinced Twardon that I was taking them to a girlfriend, implying that I planned to give them to her in exchange for certain favors. Twardon thought this was hilarious. Instead of shooting me he let me go."

Another time, Norman says, he was able to keep Twardon from having him killed by promising to deliver large quantities of coffee beans. "The Germans were crazy for fresh-brewed coffee and would do anything for it," Norman recalls. "They would have sold their souls—if they'd had souls—for a cup of coffee."

"And so coffee beans saved your life?" I ask, astonished.

"Yes, yes, can you imagine? It is so crazy, but this is what happened. This Polish girl, the German postmaster's mistress, she got angry at me for cutting into a line of people waiting for skim milk. Actually, I didn't cut in line because it was prearranged that since I was to collect it for those of us who were slave laborers, I was not to wait in the line, wasting time.

"Well, this young woman made a big scene. She wouldn't hear my explanation. She cursed at me and dumped the milk onto the ground. She went around claiming that I said things that I didn't. She made such a scene that by the end of the day Twardon had given orders that I was to be shot the next day."

Norman sighs. He touches some papers on his desk, moving them around absently. And then he tells me of another twist of fate.

"I was warned about Twardon by a Polish policeman named Patek. This man had tried to help me on several occasions, and I was always puzzled. Why me? Finally, he told me that I looked exactly like his son, who had been killed in battle in 1939. He and his wife had this idea they should keep watch over me and try to protect me, even though I was a complete stranger and a Jew."

So Patek came to Norman and warned him, urging him to

run away. Norman, however, chose not to do that. "When someone ran away," he explains, "the Germans would kill ten people in his place. I knew this would probably include my friends in the labor camp and almost certainly my brother Leibush."

The next morning Norman was dragged to the police station. "All the time, I was trying to talk my way out of it. When we got to the station, the two Polish policemen who had been assigned to kill me handed me a shovel and told me to start digging."

Norman sees that I cannot hide my revulsion.

"Yes, it is disgusting," Norman says, then continues: "I thought, *What should I do? Throw a shovelful of dirt in their eyes?* While I dug, I just kept talking. By now I was knee-deep. Suddenly, I had a wild idea—I asked to see Krzysia Kotulecka, one of Twardon's secretaries, claiming I had an important message for her. I persuaded one of them to get her, and she returned with him. By now the hole in the ground was waist-high. I was running out of time! I convinced Krzysia that I must see Twardon, that I had important information."

"Why would they listen to you?" I ask him.

"Because they were scared for themselves. They took me to see Twardon. Oh, he was enraged to see that I was still alive. It's a good thing I'm a fast talker because I just kept talking as fast as I could until I hit on something that got his attention. I mentioned that I could provide him with an endless supply of coffee beans. Actually, this was true. I had a hundred kilos of coffee beans, which my father had hidden with a peasant when the war broke out."

"And you persuaded Twardon?"

"Yes, and it saved my life. All I can say now is, thank God he loved coffee. I was able to keep him happy for weeks by getting a small amount of coffee beans at a time. Obviously, I didn't want to give him the whole amount at once."

Norman's story, at the moment, seems funny but then takes a perverse twist. "The Germans never wasted anything, not even an open grave," Norman says. "So Twardon immediately ordered the arrest of a man who had complained that Twardon's dog had bit him. He was a Gentile, a well-off and prominent member of the community. He was dragged to 'my' grave, shot on sight, and buried there.

"The thing is," Norman adds, "my friends back at the labor camp heard those shots and assumed it was I, poor Naftali, who had been killed. When I walked up to them a few minutes later, they screamed and cried for joy!"

Once again, Norman had cheated death. But winter was coming, and it was obvious to all the young men that soon there would be no work to do. After they had torn down the houses, they were made to straighten out the river—literally, from one end of town to the other, all by hand. It wasn't hard to guess what the Germans might do once they had no use for them anymore.

Norman started to organize an escape. What they would need, if somehow they did manage to escape, were friendly Poles as allies. "I spoke to a Polish woman I knew, a widow named Mrs. Kotulova, and asked her to obtain false papers for me and Leibush," Norman recalls. "This was a huge risk, but I felt we had no choice. Fortunately, she agreed to talk to Monsignor Dunajecki, who had been the parish priest for over twenty years.

"He was a tall, quiet, dignified man, about sixty-five years old, but other than that I knew nothing about him. Like most Jews, I had no contact with the Catholic Church. I was aware that some priests in Poland were openly anti-Semitic. When

I saw the monsignor walk down the street, I would cross to the other side and look away."

Mrs. Kotulova kept her word. She met with the monsignor, who had all of the birth records for the parish. The monsignor moved quickly. "By the next evening, I held in my hands the birth certificate of Tadeusz Jan Jadach, a Roman Catholic Pole born in 1918 in Werynia, who had been killed at the front in 1939. I had known him. We were in the same class in public school in Kolbuszowa and resembled each other."

"And Leibush?"

"He was now the very happy owner of the birth certificate of someone named Ludwig Kunefal, a Capucin born in 1904, who had died in 1936."

When Norman asked Mrs. Kotulova how they could thank the monsignor, she said the monsignor had suggested they give fifty zlotys to the church for a special Mass. They did this immediately. "It was kind of funny in a way," Norman says with a laugh. "I never thought I would see the day when I would be paying for a Mass!"

Several days later, the monsignor sent word that he wanted to meet with Norman and Leibush. A meeting was arranged at Mrs. Kotulova's house.

"We were at a loss for words when we met him," Norman recalls. "He said, 'I am Proboszcz Dunajecki, and I am pleased to meet you both.' The meeting felt like a celebration—which it was!"

At one point, however, the monsignor took Norman aside and said that now that he had met them, he could see that Leibush did not speak Polish well enough to use the new ID without getting caught. Norman thinks the monsignor didn't want to say this in front of Leibush because he didn't want to hurt Leibush's feelings.

"I took the birth certificate for Leibush and, in front of the monsignor, ripped it up," Norman says. "I didn't want him to worry that we would use it. Not only would it endanger Leibush; it could implicate the monsignor if we were caught. Leibush would have to depend on me and my new identity."

Before they left, Norman says, the monsignor became very pensive and serious. "You know, Tadeusz," he said, using Norman's new name, "I have been a priest here in Kolbuszowa for more than twenty years, and I never really got to know a single Jew. I never had any dealings with Jewish organizations, and I never had the slightest idea about what was going on in the Jewish community. I never even met your rabbi. Now, in view of what's happened to the Jews here, I deeply regret not having made the effort to know your people better. What's most upsetting to me is the realization that I could have saved scores of Jewish children by placing them among my parishioners; it would have been an easy thing to do. But no one said anything to me, and I myself have been remiss for neglecting to learn what was happening. I can't tell you how sorry I am."

They shook hands, and the monsignor wished them luck. Then he made the sign of the cross over the two young Jewish men as they said good-bye.

Many years later, Norman finally was able to learn more about Monsignor Dunajecki. The monsignor, it turns out, was from a family of German colonists who had come to Poland, to an area then known as Galicia, about two hundred years earlier. At the time of the monsignor's birth, in 1882, it was part of Austria. The family name was Schmidt, and they were farmers. When he became a priest, he changed his name to Dunajecki, a reflection of the fact that his hometown was located on the Dunajec River.

With his new ID in hand, Norman had a chance—his first real opportunity perhaps to survive. It came just at the right moment, for at the slave labor camp, the men could see that time was running out. A Polish construction crew arrived and began digging ditches in the woods in Nowa-Wies, near the town. Ditches? For what? For mass graves?

Norman says his usual strategy was to "stay put." Asked to expand on that, he says, "I believed that as a survival technique, unless you were in direct danger, you were generally safer where you were. But at that point, even I believed it was time to go. I was not going to just stay and be killed like a sitting duck."

And so Norman planned an escape and invited the others to join. Some, he said, were just too afraid, or too weary, to chance it. But on the night of November 18, 1942, about fifty-five men were prepared. They had done what they could to make contacts so they had a place to stay temporarily, Norman says. Arrangements were made with promises of money that had been hidden.

"The night of the escape, the tension in the camp was terrible," Norman says. He remembers thinking, *Perhaps this is how the children of Israel felt on the night they fled Egypt.*

One by one, the men sneaked out of the labor camp. This part, Norman says, was not too hard; inmates there weren't guarded as closely as they would have been at a death camp. Norman decided to be the last one to go. He climbed over the fence and ran.

At 2:00 A.M. the Germans started searching. About ten of Norman's comrades were found hiding and shot immediately. Within a week, twenty more were killed. Those who survived, Norman says, knew it was only a matter of time before they were found, too.

"We had to get away from our hiding places and into the deep forest," he tells me. "We already knew there was a group of Jews hiding in the woods, and I hoped we could join them.

I knew a local Pole, a fellow named Franek, who had delivered merchandise to my father's store before the war. I heard he had been in contact with the Jews in the woods and asked if he would contact them for me. He did this for me, and the news was good: We were welcome to join them.

"The next thing I did was contact a peasant by the name of Bronek, who was said to have access to weapons," Norman continues. "From him, I bought my first firearm, a long-barreled 9 millimeter handgun, brand new, with 120 rounds of ammunition."

Several nights later, they made their connection and were introduced to their new "family" in the forest. They were taken there by a man named Lyba Leibowicz, who had owned a grocery store in a nearby village and had done business with Norman's father and with Leibush, Norman says.

"Lyba was also a trapper by trade, an unusual occupation for a Jew, but it was a huge advantage to us all. He knew the forest well. I will tell you, though, he was an odd fellow. He had this huge nose, as big as Pinocchio's. In the woods, he moved like a deer or a fox or some other animal. He was able to see in the dark and to move in total silence. We walked a long time in total darkness that first night. Leibush and I had no idea where we were or where we were going. I hung onto Lyba's jacket, and Leibush held onto mine!"

Norman makes this episode sound comical, these many years later. It is part of his gift, to laugh at the situation, and he makes me laugh, too.

"Suddenly, after what seemed like hours, Lyba paused and made a whistling sound," Norman continues. "Looking closely in the dark, I could see the limbs of a small pine tree begin to move. A man's face appeared. Without a word, we followed Lyba through a hidden passageway and into a secret underground bunker."

They found about forty people in the bunker, all Jews who had fled into the forest when they saw other Jews being rounded up and taken away. The group was already too large for the bunker. They had been planning to build a new bunker, and with the arrival of Norman and Leibush, it was necessary to build two more, Norman says.

"This was an incredible project," Norman recalls with a groan. "We couldn't alert anyone to our presence, so we had to hide all the dirt! What we did was carry it further into the forest. And we didn't dare use any of the wood nearby for support beams. We didn't dare break a single twig. It would call attention to us."

They spent the daylight hours hiding in the bunker and sleeping. At night, they did all of the chores. Anyone with local contacts among the Polish peasants would go to get supplies.

"Were you afraid the Germans would come after you, so far into the forest?" I ask.

"No, not really. The Germans never ventured deep into the forest, but the local peasants did," Norman recalls. "The peasants were not allowed by the Germans to keep firearms, so we felt we had an advantage over them. We built up a small arsenal, just in case. Twenty-four hours a day, I wore a leather belt that secured my long-barreled revolver, two hand grenades, an ax, a flashlight, a bayonet, a wooden spoon, and 120 rounds of ammunition."

The unofficial leader of the group was a man named Pinyeh Frohlich, who had been a forester for a rich Jewish family named Vang. "He had a talent for settling disputes within the group," Norman explains. He had brought with him his wife, Feige. Their daughter, age fifteen, was working as a shepherd for a peasant family who believed she was Catholic. (Another daughter had been killed, but Norman says he never learned the details.) Feige's brother was

Avrum Seiden, a man nicknamed Langer Avrum, which means Tall Avrum, who also had brought along his wife. There was a woman in her seventies, nicknamed Grandma, who did all the cooking, Norman says. Other than the three women, the rest of the group was made up of grown men— and one small child, the little son of Tall Avrum and his wife.

"We called him Tarzan because he was born in the woods and ran around naked," Norman says. "We all loved him. Leibush, who had lost his children, and I, who had lost my nieces and nephews, enjoyed so much being around this happy little child. It also made things seem more normal to us, to have a little, innocent child running about."

Everything was routine for two months, Norman recalls. Then one day in January 1943, several members of the group, including Norman and Leibush, returned to the bunker and found that disaster had struck. They approached, guns drawn, for Lyba sensed something was wrong.

This is how Norman describes the scene:

"They were all dead. Polish peasants killed them. Worst of all was the sight of little Tarzan, lying beside his mother, both lifeless. Such pity for anyone I have never felt as I did when Tall Avrum, who was with us, knelt down and held Tarzan and kissed his wife.

"We put the dead in the bunker and left quickly. We thought the murderers might still be around. Three days later, we returned and held a brief funeral service.

"I guess it would have been easier to just bury them in the bunker, but we didn't even consider it," Norman says softly. "We couldn't stand the idea that they would be buried in that bunker, where they had hidden for so many months. It would have been immoral."

Chapter Twelve

THE MASQUERADE

Do you want to hear something peculiar?" Amalie asks, laughing softly. "The Germans I worked for called me *Sonnenstrahl*. It means 'Little Sunshine.'"

It's Amalie's turn again to continue her story. "Of course," she adds, "on the inside I was sad, frightened, and alone. At night, my pillow was wet with tears."

It seems clear to me that Amalie considers Norman's ordeal to be more harrowing than hers. She says, "It was harder for him than for me." When pressed, she lowers her voice and confides her reasoning: "I didn't see any of my loved ones killed in front of me, and he did."

But what about the fact that she was a woman alone with all the perils that entailed? Suddenly, it seems obvious that in some ways it *was* harder for her. She seems a little surprised and maybe a little proud, as if she had always considered Norman's story more worthy than hers without questioning the assumption.

"It is true that being a woman, I had to worry about the motivation of men," she says.

Perhaps surprisingly, rape or molestation by German soldiers was not an overwhelming concern. "Some Jewish women were raped, of course, but it wasn't common," Amalie says. "When Celia and I were forced to work at Gestapo headquarters, naturally, we were terrified that we

125

would be forced to be concubines, but the Germans had strict rules that their soldiers could not touch a Jewish girl, and this was largely enforced."

Essentially, Jewish women were so revolting in the eyes of the Germans that they were, paradoxically, saved from being raped by them, Amalie explains to me.

Amalie discusses these sensitive points with grace and directness. The next subject throws her a bit off balance. "As a beautiful woman," I ask, "what part do you think your looks played in your ability to survive?"

"There were many beautiful Jewesses," she says modestly. "Luck was more important in terms of survival. I was luckier than many people."

She adds, however, that if she had looked more typically Jewish, she would never have been able to masquerade. "As I told you before, people used to say that Jews had sad eyes, and mine are shining and happy, so that worked in my favor. And like my mother, I had perfect teeth, and I'm sure having a nice smile didn't hurt."

The topic seems to make her uncomfortable. She is blushing slightly. "It is true, there is no denying it," she adds. "It is part of my story." She shrugs her shoulders. "This is the way it was."

There were encounters when the sheltered nineteen-year-old had to defend her virtue. At one boardinghouse where she lived, the landlady tried to entice her into prostitution, offering to pose as a madam and split the money. Amalie, horrified, declined.

Not long after, she mentioned in passing to the landlady that she needed a new pair of rubber boots. "Later that night I found a man in my bed," Amalie says. "I screamed and threw him out, and the next morning the landlady said, 'Well, you said you needed a new pair of boots.' As if that was the way to get them!"

Still, many of the men she encountered were gentlemen. But even those who helped her might have done so because they were infatuated with her and not simply from the goodness of their hearts. The German businessman who helped her get the construction-company job later asked her to marry him, as did Mundek, her guardian angel. And, of course, so had the Hungarian count, several years earlier.

Amalie is aware of these complexities, the messy and conflicted motivations. But her discomfort at discussing the topic seems to go beyond mere embarrassment. Could it be that she feels guilty that her beauty helped her?

"I am a little surprised to say it aloud, but that is true. It makes me a little ashamed, although I did nothing wrong."

She had other qualities and abilities that increased her chances of survival. She notes, for example, the fact that she spoke Polish and German fluently, while most Jewish people spoke only Yiddish. And the fact that she was self-confident, tenacious, and able to think quickly.

Nowhere was that more evident than that she was able to masquerade as a Christian. Amalie didn't even know the basic fundamentals of Christianity. There was no one to teach her, no one to ask, and no way of getting books about it without calling attention to herself.

"So, exactly how did you do it?"

"I just took it one step at a time. Every time something came up, I managed to bluff my way through it."

There was the Ukrainian officer who, during the raid at the boardinghouse in Lvov, demanded that she recite the Lord's Prayer. She told him, "I don't know it—my family was never religious."

He didn't believe her and dragged her to Gestapo headquarters. On the way, he said, "Why don't you admit that you're Jewish? If you do, I promise I'll let you go."

Realizing that she would never leave the building alive, she took the chance. "All right," she responded. "I am Jewish. Go ahead, shoot me; have another innocent victim on your conscience."

The Ukrainian officer, she recalls, turned purple with rage. "You can go to hell! Run along. Someone else will get you sooner or later."

Then there was the moment when she arrived at the railroad station in Cracow and a Polish policeman was suspicious. "There was a raid under way for Poles who didn't have valid working papers," Amalie recalls. "I was singled out."

"Tell me how many divinities there are," he demanded.

"There is one God," she said.

"And what else?"

"And he has one Son."

"And what about the Holy Ghost?"

"What about it?"

"How many apostles are there?"

"Ten."

"Try twelve."

Amalie says she could see no way out this time. "I felt death coming—I completely resigned myself. I thought, *Okay, so now I will die; I did not succeed. I will join my loved ones in heaven.* I said the prayer of the dying. I then felt numb. Then I felt very light. I was standing there as if my soul had already left me."

A tall Gestapo officer with a huge German shepherd dog strolled over. "My feet were glued to the ground. The Polish police mocked me. They said, 'Move, Jewess, move!' I had a little handbag that they looked through. I pretended I didn't

Norman Salsitz (Naftali Saleschutz) in 1928 (age 8) in Kolbuszowa, Poland.

Photos courtesy of the family except as noted.

☛ Four generations, Stanislawow, Poland, 1930. *Clockwise (from l.):* Pepka Petranker; Pepka's mother, Frieda Petranker; Frieda's mother, Ryfka Genger; Ryfka's mother, Shprinca (Landau) Honigsberg.

☛ Amalie with her paternal grandparents, sisters, and cousins in Delatyn, 1929. *Sitting (l. to r.):* Celia Petranker and three cousins ("Avrumcie's daughter, Perel's son, Perel's daughter"). *Second row (l. to r.):* Pepka and Amalie. *Standing (l. to r.):* "Hershel—Perel's son," Josef Petranker, "Celia Petranker/Berlin," Chana Lea Petranker, Leo Petranker.

Amalie and her family, Stanislawow, Poland 1930 *(l. to r.):* Celia, father David, Pepka, mother Frieda, and Amalie.

Celia Petranker, Amalie's little sister, in 1937 (age 14).

Norman with his classmates, 1933. *Top (l. to r):* David Fridenreich, Szlomo Grunstein, and Leizer Bloch. *Bottom (l. to r.):* Noa Hutner and Norman Salsitz (Naftali Saleschutz).

Norman with the extended Saleschutz family, Kolbuszowa, Poland 1934. *Bottom (l. to r):* Norman (Naftali), nephew Shulim (Leibush's son), sister Rachel, and niece Shaindel (Gela's daughter). *Middle (l. to r.):* Al (Avrum), mother Esther, father Isak, sister Gela, and Ruben Weinstein (Gela's husband). *Top (l. to r.):* sister Matel, Szaja David (Malcia's husband), sister Malcia, brother David, Chancia (Leibush's wife), brother Leibush, and sister Leiba. The photo was taken to mark the visit from America of brother Avrum. (The photo of David, who was in Palestine, was added by the family at a later date to make the portrait complete.)

Amalie with her family in
Stanislawow, Poland, 1937
(l. to r.): Amalie, mother Frieda,
Menashe (an adopted brother),
Celia, father David, and Pepka.

Professors with their
pupils. Stanislawow
Hebrew School, 1929.
Amalie is in front row,
second from right.

Three of Norman's five
sisters with their
children in the ghetto
at Kolbuszowa, Poland,
1941.

◀ Father Dunajecki, the priest who provided false papers for Norman. His ancestors were German colonists who had lived in Poland for more than 200 years.

➥ Norman with one of his young nieces and two young nephews, Kolbuszowa ghetto, 1941 *(l. to r.):* Shulim Saleschutz (Leibush's son); Blimcia Lische (Malcia's daughter); Henoch Kornfeld (Leiba's son), and Norman. Note the armband, the Jewish star, which Shulim proudly displays. He has just turned 12, the age at which children in Kolbuszowa ghetto were forced to begin wearing the armband. He misunderstood the significance of it, thinking it is a rite of passage or "badge of adulthood."

Amalie in Krakow, 1945.

Norman as a Russian partisan.

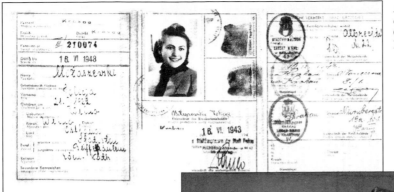

Amalie's identification card as the Roman Catholic Felicia Milaszewska.

Amalie and Norman, Poland, February 1945, shortly after they met.

Norman in Munich, 1946.

A traveling pass issued by Landkommissar Twardon to Naftali Saleschutz (Norman) in 1942.

Dancing at Leo Petranker's wedding. New York City, 1950.

Amalie with Esther, April 1957.

Norman and Amalie take Esther to summer camp. New Jersey, 1966.

Esther's wedding day. Norman and Amalie with the bride, Esther, and the groom, Bruce Dezube. June 19, 1977.

Two wonderful visitors from Poland (l. to r.): Norman, Mrs. Kazimir Jerzenicki (who helped Amalie during the war), Amalie, and Stashka Hodur Bardzik (who helped Norman). Atlantic City, October 1987. The two Polish Christian women accepted Norman and Amalie's invitation to come to the United States as their guests.

Esther meets two people who aided her parents during the war (l. to r.): Esther, Stashka Hodur Bardzik (who helped Norman), Mundek Abrahamowicz-Sultanski (who helped Amalie), and Amalie. Poland, 1974.

Amalie and Norman in Jerusalem, December 1991. "If there had been a state of Israel during World War II, my family would have survived the war," Amalie says.

◄ Esther and Bruce's three sons: Dustin, Aaron, and Michael Dezube. September 1993.

◄ Celebrating grandson Aaron Dezube's bar mitzvah. Newton, Massachusetts, January 27, 2001. *Standing (l. to r.)*: Michael Dezube, Dr. Bruce Dezube, Dustin Dezube, Aaron, Esther Salsitz Dezube. Seated: grandparents Norman and Amalie.

Photo by Jim Webber

◄ The wedding Amalie and Norman never had. On October 22, 1995, Norman and Amalie celebrated their 50th wedding anniversary, Norman's 75th birthday (May 6), and the 50th anniversay of the end of World War II *(l. to r.)*: Pepka, Norman, Amalie, Esther, Dustin (grandson), and Esther's husband, Dr. Bruce Dezube. In front of Amalie, grandsons Aaron and Michael.

❙ Amy Hill Hearth, below left, with Norman and Amalie at Aaron Dezube's bar mitzvah. Newton, Massachusetts, January 27, 2001.

Photo by Jim Webber

understand German—only the Polish intelligentsia knew German. So a Polish policeman interpreted when the German questioned me. I said I had a sick aunt, and I was on my way to visit her. He asked, 'Where does she live?'"

Amalie catches her breath. "Well, you know how in America there is an Elm Street or a Broad Street in every city? Well, in Poland, most cities had a Mickiewicz Street named after the famous Polish poet. So I told them, 'My aunt lives on Mickiewicz Street.'"

For reasons she says she will never understand, she was let go on the orders of the Gestapo officer. *"Los, das ist noch ein Kind,"* he said. It means, "Forget it; she's just a child."

Amalie shakes her head at the memory. "I could hardly move," she adds. "I thought it was a trick. I expected the dog to be let loose as I walked away, and that it would tear me to pieces. I didn't believe I was alive. I have no explanation, except that for some reason God wanted me to live."

After these two incidents, Amalie says, she realized that many people thought she was far younger than her nineteen years. She continued to wear her hair in braids and, when questioned, played the role of the pretty, saucy adolescent.

In addition to the constant harassment by the police, both Polish and German, Amalie had to keep up appearances among her newfound Gentile friends, such as Kazia. She attended Easter services because not doing so would have attracted attention. When asked why she didn't sing the hymns at the service, Amalie says that she turned it into a joke, claiming that she couldn't carry a tune and didn't want to ruin Easter services for everyone.

Most precarious, Amalie says, was the time of her hospitalization for the abscess that developed on her neck. What on earth might she say under anesthesia? She sought out a young nurse at the hospital whom she suspected was Jewish. The woman denied being Jewish, but nevertheless agreed to stay by Amalie's side in the recovery room, lest she say something that might give her away.

As if that wasn't bad enough, the hospital chaplain, a Catholic priest, showed up at her bedside on the morning of the operation to hear confession.

Once again, she relied on charm, humor, and her adolescent appearance to finagle her way out of it.

"Oh, father, you don't really think I'm going to die, do you?" she said, giggling. Instead of confession, they ended up having a nice conversation, and he sang a beautiful song to her.

The memory of the handsome priest singing the beautiful song brings a smile to Amalie's face. "He was not a bad fellow," she says. "It was actually kind of funny when you think about it. A nice Jewish girl being asked to give confession!"

The other encounters have left deep scars, however. This is particularly true of the incident at the Cracow train station, when the Gestapo officer let her go. "I can still feel the sensation of turning and walking away, fully expecting that he would let the dog loose to tear me limb from limb or just shoot me in the back."

Why he did not is just another mystery, one more unanswered and unanswerable question. Amalie sighs a deep, long sigh and sits down wearily at the kitchen table, straightening the day's copy of the *Newark Star-Ledger*.

"Masquerading was very, very hard to do," she says finally. "That is why more people didn't try it, and most of the ones who did were caught and shot on sight or sent to the extermination camps."

Although the little Jewish girl from Stanislawow had been

succeeding at her double life, she secretly had made an important decision. If the Germans won the war, she planned to kill herself.

"I knew I could keep it up for a while," she says quietly, "but I decided that life was not worth living if it meant pretending all the time or living a lie for the rest of my life."

I nod my head in agreement. This, I can understand.

Chapter Thirteen

LIVING "HOUR-BY-HOUR"

It has been snowing. When I arrive on this day, I make the mistake of announcing cheerily that I love the first snowfall of the year.

Norman, however, hates the snow. "Maybe for you it is a nice thing. It brings back happy memories of being a child and playing with your brothers and sister," he says, sounding a little grumpy, "but for me, well obviously, it reminds me of living in the forest. It reminds me of the war. It reminds me of that bunker."

And Tarzan, no doubt. And everything else.

"Did I ever tell you that I like Christmas?" Norman asks me suddenly. He is smiling and I brace myself for a joke, but he's not joking this time.

"In the woods, Christmas Eve was the best day of the year," he explains, "because the Poles would fast—you know, starve themselves—and then eat this gigantic meal, called Posnik, late in the evening before they went to Mass at midnight. They had eleven different dishes. Of course, they never finished it all. They put it out for the dogs.

"Now, at one house, I knew the dog. The dog was my friend. On Christmas Eve, I shared with him what I got. Then I went back to the forest, and we had a feast.

"So this, for me, is why I like Christmas Eve."

His story leaves me speechless. Finally, I ask him, "What

did you do after the bunker was raided? Where did you go?"

"Well, obviously, we had no choice but to move further into the woods. We moved to a swampland, but even there we were not safe," Norman says, a flash of concern crossing his face at the memory. "The peasants, they were still hunting us. We knew it was peasants who killed Tarzan and the others because they used crude weapons, like pitchforks, axes, and knives. Germans would have used guns. Maybe these peasants thought we would avenge our friends, so they wanted to finish us all off."

More than ever, he explains, the Jewish group was very dependent on the few friendly peasants in the villages nearby. At night, those who had contacts would cautiously visit the farms and houses where people had helped them before. They were given food and supplies, sometimes for payment, sometimes for free. The group also built snares to catch animals, mostly rabbits, to keep from starving.

Norman had left money and valuables for safekeeping with various Polish families when he and his family were temporarily moved to the Rzeszow ghetto. "Now that I needed it, they were surprised to see that I had survived and had come to get my things," Norman says, adding, "and some of them weren't too happy about it, either."

In one case, Norman recalls, he was nearly killed when he came to retrieve his money. "One storekeeper and two other men attacked me when I arrived at his house to collect what I had left with him," Norman says. "I had my gun and two men with me, so when they attacked us, I shot and killed one of the attackers."

"You killed one?"

"Yes, I killed him," Norman replies bluntly, "and we escaped back to the forest with my money."

"Oh." It is hard to imagine this elderly man, this sensitive soul who brakes for squirrels crossing the road, killing another person.

"We moved around so much now, we abandoned the two new bunkers and decided not to build any more," Norman says. "At night, when we were tired, we cut down branches of spruce trees and made beds on the snow. I used to dream of having a cup of hot tea. You cannot imagine such cold."

"What kept you going? How could you stand it?"

Norman smiles one of his mischievous smiles. "The desire to see the Germans lose the war and to take revenge. Every time I felt like giving up I thought how much I would love to see the day that the tables would turn. I wasn't going to miss that, if it happened."

The other motivation was more personal. "I thought often of my parents' last wishes for me," Norman explains somberly. "They expected me to keep trying to survive. They believed that if anyone could make it, it was me, their youngest son. And I told myself, 'Someday I will tell the story of what happened to them, and I must live in order to do that. Otherwise, the Germans will rewrite our history.' "

The deep forests of Poland, especially in winter, were as cruel and merciless as the Germans. "This was not an easy thing to do, to live like this, with no permanent shelter," Norman says. "We lived hour by hour. You rest when you can; you eat when you can. You look after yourself and your comrades. It is like a team. One man helps the other. Resilience is a must. Your situation changes in a flash, and you must respond quickly. You learn to adapt."

"For example?"

"Well, for example, I carried with me a wooden spoon. When the group would make a soup or stew of whatever we had, I found out that you don't get your share of the good parts with a spoon when everyone else is using their fingers!"

Norman grins. "You do what you have to do."

He then describes how the situation, already almost unbearable, worsened further:

"We had enough problems trying to keep out of the hands of the Germans and the Poles. Then a third enemy came onto the scene. This was the Armia Krajowa or Home Army and known as the AK, the nationalist Polish underground with headquarters in London. As the Germans began to lose the war, the AK began to flourish. AK groups began to roam the forests and proved just as deadly to us as the Germans or the Polish peasants!"

"The AK went after the Jews, too?"

"Yes, they did. The head of the AK gave an order in September 1943 to all units that they should kill 'all Jewish Bolshevik bandits,' which was widely interpreted to mean any Jew on the run," Norman explains.

He describes the following incident:

"Thank God for the very few peasants who did help us. There was one man in particular, Jan Hodur, who lived in a house by the forest. He and his wife, Stefka, had seven children. They were the poorest people I had ever seen. He was a farmer, but the land was not good. He had to support the family by illegally cutting wood in the forest and selling it to people in the town.

"Stefka, his wife, was one of the nicest people I ever met. She would boil my clothing for me, killing the lice that plagued us and drove us nearly crazy. I gave her money that I had stashed away and asked her to buy some necessities for us. It was a nice arrangement. She got some money, and we got to stay alive!

"One of the seven children was a daughter, Stashka, the

eldest, who was sixteen. Time and again, I was able to rely on Stashka. She literally risked her life for me.

"One day Lyba and I had arranged to get some loaves of bread from a peasant. We would leave him money for it and pick it up one week later. Unfortunately for us, this man had gone to the local AK leader, who was visiting at Stashka's house, and informed him that two Jews would be showing up that night. It was arranged that two armed men would intercept us and kill us.

"Stashka overheard the conversation, and as soon as it turned dark, she hid in the bushes, waiting in the deep snow for four hours until we arrived. It is a wonder she did not freeze to death. I will never forget the sight of her climbing out of the bushes. She told us to run away quickly. I kissed her frozen hands, and Lyba and I ran back into the forest."

Norman falls silent. "I wonder why she was so helpful," I say to him.

"Well, years later, I asked her why she did this brave thing, and she said it was because I was a human being and she simply wanted to help me. But I also learned that she thought I was handsome and had a crush on me! So maybe that is part of the reason, too."

Although his life had once again been saved at the last second, Norman was by no means out of danger. "Now the AK was aware that we were alive and would be looking for us," he says grimly.

But then there was some good news. Norman learned that the local commander was one of his best boyhood friends, a man named Stashek. Stashek's brother, Yashek, was a contributor to two underground newspapers, *Na Posterunku* (On Guard) and *Wiesci Rzeszowskie* (News of the Rzeszow Region).

"I had sat next to Stashek in school year after year,"

Norman says, "and this gave me new hope. I thought that as the local AK leader, he might protect us. Maybe he would even take us into his organization. After all, we had a common enemy, the Germans, and we were willing to fight. At this time, 65 of the original 125 of us from the forest group were still alive." Norman was now the commander because the original leader had been killed.

It took several weeks to make the contact since the organization worked so secretly, Norman explains, but in January 1944 word finally came that Stashek would see him and Leibush. They walked for hours in deep snow until they reached the estate where Stashek and his brother were to meet them at a stable.

"Oh, it was a joyful reunion!" Norman says. "Stashek threw his arms around me the moment he saw me. His welcome was so warm and friendly that it almost made me cry. He called out to me, 'Naftali, I'm so happy to see you! I'm really delighted we're going to work together. You'll see, we'll go out and kill Germans; we will pay them back for everything they've done to your people and to mine.'"

Stashek, Norman says, asked them to stay at the stable, directing them to a secret compartment that was about eight feet wide. It was hidden behind a secret door beneath a trough. They were told to relax and given clean clothes. A little while later they shared some vodka and a pot of stew with meat and potatoes.

"Leibush and I felt like we were in heaven, but we were also uneasy," Norman says. "It seemed too good to be true."

Later, when Stashek's brother, Yashek, came back, Norman says he really began to have doubts. "Yashek kept his right hand in his pocket while he was talking to us," Norman says gravely. "This is the posture of a man hiding a weapon."

It was a Tuesday, the day that the underground newspaper

was published, and Norman asked Yashek for the latest news. His answer, Norman says, was very odd: "News?" Yashek said, sounding distracted. "I forget."

Leibush was not too concerned, but Norman was extremely wary. "The next morning Stashek appeared in our hideout, still perfectly pleasant," he recalls. "He left, then returned with Yashek, who was carrying the best breakfast we had seen in years: hard-boiled eggs, borscht, bread with butter. Eating all that wonderful food, I began to second-guess myself."

About three in the afternoon, Stashek came back with a German newspaper *Krakawer Zeitung*. Norman says, "We rejoiced because the paper predicted that the war might be over in three months."

Stashek shouted, "My God, three months!" and put his hands on Norman's shoulders, saying, "Naftali, as soon as the war is over, we'll become big wheels. You'll see."

"All I wish is that the war would end," Norman says he replied.

Stashek, according to Norman, then said, "Naftali, lend me your flashlight for a minute." Norman handed it to him. Suddenly, the kerosene lamp that was the only light went out. It was completely dark.

Norman tells me that the next few moments will be etched into his mind until the day he dies. This is how he describes what happened:

"I heard four shots—three shots in quick succession, then one more. I felt dizzy and fell backward. I thought, *If this is the end, so be it. I'm tired of it all*. Then something deep inside me protested, and I thought, *Wait a minute. If I'm going to die, so should he!*

"I never took my gun and holster off, even when bathing. So I had my gun. As I lay there on the ground, I pointed my gun into the darkness and pulled the trigger. But my finger seemed frozen. I didn't realize it was injured. Struggling, I used another finger to finally fire the gun. In the glare I saw Yashek standing in the entrance with his pistol drawn. Stashek was standing off to the side, his gun aimed straight at Leibush! Quickly, I fired two shots in Yashek's direction. After the second shot, I saw him lying across the entrance.

"In the glare I could see Stashek turn and run. As he did, I pulled the trigger again. The bullet hit him right in the back, but he kept running.

" 'Stashek, Stashek!' Leibush was shouting. 'What are you doing? Are you crazy, playing with firecrackers?'

" 'Leibush,' I shouted, 'this is not a game! This is for real.' "

Norman says he remembers the feeling of the warm blood running down his neck and also on his hand. He tried to gather up their belongings, especially the medical kit, but abandoned the effort when he heard Leibush screaming outside the stable.

"I ran to the sound of his voice and saw two men holding him down," Norman says, leaning forward in his chair as he recalls these fateful moments. "One was a school friend of mine, and the other was Bronek, the man I had bought my first gun from. Two other men—I didn't recognize them— were with Stashek, who was lying in the snow. He wasn't moving."

"How did you get out of it?" I ask, breathless.

"I sort of bluffed my way out of it," Norman says, throwing up his hands. "I pointed my revolver at the men and yelled, 'I have three bullets left in this gun, and I never miss! If you don't get the hell out of here, three of you will be dead.' "

"And then?"

"All of them, including the two men with Stashek, ran away.

"It was late in the afternoon and almost dark. Leibush and I were both wearing only underwear," Norman says. "Can you imagine? We were barefoot. I was wounded, but I didn't know how bad. We were terrified. We ran as fast as we could. I remember there was a fence; then we ran through a small brook and then through some open fields. If the AK caught us now, they'd torture us and *then* kill us, this much we knew."

When pausing momentarily to catch their breath, Norman recalls that he made a suggestion to Leibush: if they were caught, Norman would shoot as many as he could but save the last two bullets for themselves. Leibush agreed without hesitation, Norman recalls.

But Norman was not ready to give up yet. "If we could just get to Kupno, we knew of a friendly man," Norman says, "but I knew it was probably three or four kilometers away. And which way was it? I was disoriented because everything was covered with snow. I couldn't pick out any landmarks. Then I remembered there was a six o'clock bus from Rzeszow to Kolbuszowa. It was the only motor vehicle that would be traveling the road at that time of night. If we could only see the bus, I said to Leibush, then maybe we can figure out where we are."

Sure enough, two headlights soon appeared on the horizon. "We now knew where the road was and ran toward it. After a while we came upon Franek's house, a familiar place. We fled into the barn and for one brief moment felt safe, until it suddenly dawned on me that I must have left a trail of blood in the snow. We would not be safe here."

Back out into the snow they went and headed toward Kupno. Jan Shitosh was there, and he might, Norman hoped, be able to help. Jan Shitosh was a self-taught medicine man who served as the village veterinarian. "We made it to his house, and we told him that we had an altercation with some Germans and that I had shot several," Norman says, "though we didn't dare tell him it was Polish citizens—members of the AK."

"Germans!" Jan Shitosh cried. "You're placing me and my family in great danger!" Norman and Leibush stood there while the man agonized out loud. "I can't let you stay here; it's too risky. On the other hand, you're human beings, and I must help you."

Finally, Jan Shitosh got a pail of warm water and began to clean Norman's wounds, Norman recalls. " 'You have three bullet wounds in your neck and one in your right hand', he told me. He bound up the wounds and gave us some old clothes and shoes. Leibush's feet were too large for the shoes he gave us, so he had to remain barefoot."

"Barefoot? In the snow?" I couldn't help interrupting. This seemed to me as bad as being shot.

"You are right. This was very, very bad for Leibush," Norman says. "We headed for Przedborz, and when we crossed a pond that was partly frozen, Leibush's feet kept breaking through the ice. His feet were sliced to ribbons."

When at last they reached Hodur's house, Norman says, they climbed to their usual hiding place in the barn. To their surprise, they found Lyba there. Lyba hurried off to get Stashka, who came immediately and was appalled at their condition and also frightened by the bloody trail in the snow leading right up to the barn. Norman says he thought, *If only it would snow—big, fat snowflakes that would cover our tracks and protect us all!*

"I explained to Stashka that we had a shoot-out," Norman says, "but I didn't dare tell even her that it was with the AK. After all, she was a member! I told her we had a shoot-out with Germans, just as I had told Jan Shitosh. Stashka left us to go talk to her mother. Thankfully, her father was not home. He was a good man, but I'm not sure he would have been as sympathetic as the mother, who was so fond of me she called me *Nasz Tadek*, which means 'Our Teddy.'"

Before long Stashka returned with her kindhearted mother, who took one look at Norman and agreed to take him to a physician.

As soon as they left for the doctor, it began to snow.

PART TWO

Introduction

A WARNING TO THE WORLD

W hat is a Jew?"
"A Jew is someone who doesn't celebrate Christmas."

That was the extent of the knowledge that my first-grade classmates in Columbia, South Carolina, circa 1965, had about Judaism. My family had moved from the North that year, and it took some adjusting on my part. Not that I was so much more knowledgeable than my classmates. But at least my parents had actually known several Jews. In fact, I was aware that my father, during service in World War II, had made many close acquaintances, including at least two Jewish men with whom he remained lifelong friends.

I knew for a fact, for instance, that Jews did not have horns, as was widely believed in my grammar school.

Abraham H. Foxman, national director of the Anti-Defamation League, listens closely as I describe these memories to him. He laughs in a sad, ironic sort of way. "These are the seeds of the Holocaust," he says. "Ignorance and suspicion."

Mr. Foxman, a child survivor himself, has spent a lifetime trying to grapple with the Holocaust and its causes both on personal and professional levels. He is a crusader not just against anti-Semitism, but against all forms of bigotry and intolerance. Over the years, he has come to know hundreds of Holocaust survivors, including Norman and Amalie Salsitz.

At his office near the United Nations in New York City one frosty morning, Mr. Foxman takes time out from his demanding schedule to philosophize about the legacy of the Holocaust, its root causes, and its place in history. He explains to me the process, as he sees it, in which some Holocaust survivors, epitomized in many ways by Norman Salsitz, have evolved from being victims to activists.

"There's been a progression among survivors in terms of their willingness and ability to bear witness," he says. "In the early years, most clammed up. They were traumatized. They almost found it difficult to understand what it is they survived.

"After the war, there was silence. There was very little attention paid to the Holocaust," he explains. "The survivors began to build their lives; they had children. And again, there was silence.

"By the 1950s, 1960s, and 1970s, the survivors began to be heard from, but their preoccupation was to preserve towns, to bear witness to communities lost, not individuals. There are literally thousands of memorial books about lost communities.

"Then survivors, notably Elie Wiesel, began to talk to the outside world about what it was that had happened. For the first time, there was communication outside the [Jewish] community about the Holocaust.

"In the late 1970s and 1980s, two phenomena helped to push the Holocaust out into the open," he says. "The reality of mortality was one factor. The survivors began to panic that they must bear witness or it would be too late."

And the other?

"The Holocaust deniers came on the scene. It was completely traumatizing to survivors. The deniers have really flourished these last fifteen or twenty years."

This, he says, resulted in "an avalanche of testimonies" by survivors. An entire movement began in which survivors volunteered to go to schools and other public venues to share their stories.

"All of this stirred up a lot of interest in the Holocaust," Mr. Foxman says. "It also stirred up a lot of painful memories for the survivors."

Along with the pain of reliving the past, Mr. Foxman adds, is a debilitating problem: guilt.

"Most of the Holocaust survivors, in my opinion, have guilt. I know my parents struggled with it. They would ask 'Why did we survive and not the others?' I sometimes feel that way, too. Some people develop a rationale. They say, 'I survived to bear witness.'"

Mr. Foxman was what is known among Holocaust survivors as a "hidden child." His parents gave him at the age of one year and three months to his nanny when it seemed imminent that they would be sent to a death camp. Incredibly, they survived and returned home to Lithuania at the end of the war when Mr. Foxman, an only child, was five.

There was, however, no simple happy ending. The nanny refused to turn over the child. A vicious custody battle ensued, and Mr. Foxman was finally returned to his parents at age six.

"It was confusing to say the least," he says with emphasis. "My nanny fought very hard to keep from giving me back."

The nanny had been raising Mr. Foxman as a Catholic. "I had no idea I was Jewish," he says. "I believed, I *knew*, I was Catholic!" After he was returned to his parents, his father took him to both church and synagogue to help him adjust.

Mr. Foxman, a whirlwind of a man who has been speaking

quickly, suddenly pauses. "This is a difficult issue for me," he says after a moment. "She [the nanny] was, I guess, shocked that my parents survived and returned for me. She considered me to be her child."

With irony in his voice, Mr. Foxman recalls a recent trip to Germany where some students said of the Holocaust, "It's over."

"I told them, 'It's not over. It's not over for me. So it's not over for my kids. It won't be over for a couple of generations.'"

What responsibility do people of German ancestry have for what happened? Especially those born after the war ended?

"I would say there is an *obligation*, not a responsibility," Mr. Foxman replies. "In the Jewish tradition we cannot try the child for the sins of the father. But I think I have a right to ask them to face the past."

What about Christians in general?

"The fact is," Mr. Foxman says matter-of-factly, "that many of these people, these perpetrators, committed these atrocities and then went to church on Sundays.

"Why did Christianity tolerate this?" he asks rhetorically. "Part of the answer is anti-Semitism. Religious leaders since the Inquisition have fed anti-Semitism." But that, he adds forcefully, is why "this pope [Pope John Paul II] is so important. He has gone further than any other in two thousand years to make things better between Christians and Jews."

Still, Mr. Foxman fears for the future. "Anti-Semitism is resilient," he says. "There is a predisposition in history of mistreatment of Jews. First it was, 'You can't live among us as Jews.' Then it was, 'You can't live among us.' Finally, it was, 'You can't live.'"

One of the paradoxical lessons of the Holocaust, Mr.

Foxman believes, is that it is not just about death but also about life. "How much these people wanted to live!" he exclaims, waving his right arm in the air for emphasis. "Jewish tradition places tremendous value on life. To remove oneself from life, in Judaism, is a sin. This, in part, explains the survivors' tenacity."

The burden falls on the survivors, like Norman and Amalie, to warn the world that it must take care not to repeat its most tragic and savage event. But now the survivors are old, and their numbers are dwindling. There is great anxiety in the tightly knit world of survivors, Mr. Foxman says, about what will happen when the last eyewitness is buried.

Who will tell the story when they are gone?

Chapter Fourteen

THE NEXT GENERATION

It is late afternoon on a crisp autumn day in the charming town of Newton Centre, Massachusetts, just outside Boston. Inside a pleasing house on a street called Meadowbrook, a youthful-looking woman is struggling to prepare a roast beef for the oven with her left hand while answering repeated phone calls with her right. A wife and mother of three boys, she runs her own successful law practice in Boston.

She is Esther Dezube, Norman and Amalie's daughter.

One of the boys, Aaron, the mischievous one, had permission to work on a special art project after school but has apparently decided to walk home instead of waiting for his mother to pick him up as agreed.

A series of phone calls to teachers, friends, and neighbors yields no information and leaves the woman frantic. The roast beef, ready for the oven, is left on top of the stove. She directs Dustin, fifteen, to watch over Michael, eight, while she looks for the errant Aaron, who is eleven. Into the van she goes, cell phone in hand, with the boys' golden retriever panting happily in the back.

Aaron returns before she does. When she bursts in the door later, he is prowling about the kitchen looking for a snack. He looks up at her as if to say, "Gee, Mom, what's the matter?"

Such is the life of Esther, just as it is for many American women of her generation. To catch her in a quiet moment alone is to witness a small miracle.

The real miracle is that Esther exists at all. And she is not, at all, the quintessential American mom. Beneath the facade of everyday concerns about overcooked roast beefs, law clients who need immediate advice, and boys who don't come home from school on time is a person who carries the weight of the Holocaust on her slender shoulders—one generation removed.

"I can remember very early in my life being aware that I was different from other kids," she says. "For one thing, on Sundays it seemed like every kid in the neighborhood in Springfield was visited by their grandparents. Well, I didn't have any grandparents."

She explains that at an early age she was "older" than her peers. "I was always around Holocaust survivors. My parents did not really socialize outside of other survivors. These people supported each other, helped each other live normal lives. I understand that. But I also know that for a kid to grow up around that, you become very cynical. I wouldn't call myself a lighthearted person. I laugh and like funny things, but I am not lighthearted."

Dr. Bruce Dezube, an AIDS cancer doctor affiliated with Harvard who lectures around the world, watches his wife intently while she speaks. His in-laws' experiences have had a very direct impact on his life, too.

"I have a great deal of respect for them, for what they went through," he says softly. A gentle and thoughtful man, he began working with people with AIDS "at a time [the early 1980s] when no one would touch them."

He draws a parallel between the Jews of the Holocaust and persons with AIDS in modern society. "Nobody wants them," he says. "The community considers them a scourge. Even in the medical community, people often turn their back on them. But they are people, and they deserve to be treated like human beings. I think my father-in-law and my mother-in-law made me more conscious of the importance of compassion."

Bruce is not the only one whose career choice has been affected by Norman and Amalie. "I think it's the reason I became a lawyer, and it's probably the reason I am a plaintiff's attorney and I'm very selective about my cases," Esther says. "I want to help the underdog."

She loves to draw, a talent, she's been told, that she inherited from her mother's father, David Petranker, whom, of course, she never knew. In the hallway, among her many framed paintings and drawings, is an illustration—half-finished but framed nonetheless—of an older bearded man.

"I wanted to draw a portrait of a grandfather, but I purposely didn't finish it," she says. "To me, it symbolizes the fact that my grandfather's life was only half completed at the time of his death."

It may as well be a self-portrait, for it seems to signify Esther's feelings of being incomplete as well.

"I admire my parents and I love them dearly, but when I was a child, I just wanted them to be like other kids' parents," she says, straightening the half-finished portrait on the wall, askew from the boys' pounding feet as they race about the house. "I just wanted my parents to be normal. I just wanted to be an American kid."

The boys' golden retriever, Sunshine, licks her hand. She smiles, welcoming the animal's simple act of love. "This dog is the best-behaved member of the family," she says, laughing. The dog, in fact, has been known to walk patiently about the house with the boys' pet skink (a type of lizard) on her back.

While Esther complains good-naturedly about her busy life, it seems obvious that she wouldn't want it any other way. "Growing up as an only child, I wanted a household with more activity than I had," she explains.

She sees the world differently from most Americans her age. She admits to stocking much more food in the pantry than the family needs. "In the back of my mind, I'm always thinking, *What if there's a war?* I know it's a little weird, but it's part of who I am."

And the boys, well, it is paramount to her that they be resourceful and independent, "in case it [the Holocaust] happens again someday, so that they'll be able to survive."

Wearing jeans and a casual sweater, having discarded her formal work attire, Esther seems to relax at last. The roast is back in the oven, the boys can be heard in the background, but there is relative peace.

She recalls Norman and Amalie as loving parents. "My father worked day and night when I was a child," she says, "but I have wonderful memories of him singing to me in Yiddish. And my mother—my mother was devoted to me. My mother took me everywhere she went."

Did they talk about the past?

"There are two types of survivors," she says. "My mother said little. My father never stopped talking about it.

"There was a great sense of loss," she adds, "a sense of isolation. I realized early that my parents were very hurt by life. My uncle Leo [Petranker] and his family tried very much to incorporate us into his family, so we did have family support. But it was terrible knowing that there were all these people missing from my parents' lives and mine, too. It was terrible not to have the extended family, the aunts and uncles and grandparents, that every other kid in our neighborhood seemed to have."

Esther pauses for a few moments, focusing on Sunshine, the dog, who nudges her muzzle into her hand.

Her face brightens with more pleasant thoughts. "There was a neighbor girl whose grandparents sort of 'adopted' me," she says cheerfully. "They came to see her every weekend, and I guess they felt badly for me. They even brought me along to their home in Asbury Park [at the New Jersey shore] a few times. And there was another neighbor—she was Polish and Italian, I think—who used to invite me over."

It didn't help, she says, that she was a chubby child, shy and somewhat awkward, unsure of her place in the world. That no longer seems the case. She is open and friendly and easy to like. She has her mother's pleasing good looks and her father's quick smile.

"Being the child of my parents was not an easy role to have," she says quietly. "But they are my parents and I love them no matter what."

Chapter Fifteen

A TIME FOR REFLECTION

I wanted my daughter to have a normal life," Amalie tells
me. I am back in Springfield, New Jersey, at the cream-
colored house. I have just finished telling Amalie about
my visit to Esther's. "I was so happy that she excelled in
school, that she found happiness in marriage and her three
sons, that she has a career she can be proud of."

Amalie beams when she speaks of Esther. *Thank God for
Esther,* I say to myself, *for she has brought them joy.*

"Do you know what makes me the most proud?" Amalie
asks me. "As a lawyer, she only takes cases she believes in.
She could make much more money, but she has integrity. She
knows that integrity is something you earn and it is yours,
and no one can take it from you."

After meeting Esther, I know that is true. What I can't
fathom about Esther is how she carries the weight of the
past—her parents' past—with such grace. I'm not sure I
could. But perhaps it isn't so surprising that Norman and
Amalie's offspring would be strong and resilient.

"My daughter had everything that I did not have," Amalie
says. "She had a beautiful wedding. She went to college and
graduate school. I wish I could have had those things, but it
was not to be."

If not for the war, Norman and Amalie would never have
met. Norman would have married his girlfriend, Rozia,

155

Amalie says, and she would have married a young man from her city, someone like her boyfriend, Alek.

She notes the differences between her upbringing and Norman's. "He was from a Hasidic family, very conservative, living in a small town, while I was from a progressive family in a large city. There would have been no reason for our paths to cross without the war and the Holocaust."

And Esther, of course, would not be here.

"Yes, strange to say, but I would not have Esther, of course. And who knows what would have happened? Another thing is that we almost went to Palestine, not America. This was our original plan, but the British had control and closed the borders to Jewish immigration. They were detaining Jewish immigrants in Cyprus. I said to Norman, 'I'm not going! I didn't survive the Holocaust to sit in a British camp on Cyprus!'"

But to get to the U.S., she recalls, was not easy. "You could not get here from Poland," Amalie explains. "First you had to get out of Poland and to Germany, under U.S. control after the liberation. We still had our fake ID cards, and the borders were strictly monitored. Norman went first, and the plan was that I would join him. However, when it was discovered that he was gone, I was detained in a prison in Breslau! For ten days, they held me hostage, hoping that Norman might return to look for me. Finally, they let me go, and as soon as I could, I left to join Norman."

Reunited in Germany, living temporarily in the American zone in Munich, the young couple pondered their past and their future under newly difficult circumstances. "We felt that the evil ones were all around us. Every time we heard someone speaking in German it made us cringe."

Amalie recalls those days as emotionally torturous. "On the one hand, I was elated that I had survived," she explains.

"I thought, *This is the end of the fear. I am a free person now and not a hunted one*. On the other hand, it was *so sad*. Now that the war was over and I had time for reflection, it was actually worse because I had time to think."

Without Norman, Amalie says, she isn't sure she would have made it through those difficult times. "Perhaps I would have given up and died, but Norman was a big support. He was very resilient, very resourceful. And he loved me! Even today, I need him so. It may not always seem this way, but it is so.

"Norman, he is amazing," she adds admiringly. "While we were stuck in Germany, he insisted we do things like go to the theater, even though we had almost no money to spare."

One time, he took her to see *Der Zigeunerbaron (The Gypsy Baron)*, the operetta by Johann Strauss. The young couple waited in line, but the theater ran out of tickets before they could be seated. This incident sparked a rage in Norman, which, Amalie says, illustrates how raw their feelings were at the time.

"It really incensed Norman that all of these Germans would get to enjoy the opera and we couldn't," Amalie recalls. "He found the manager, and he told him, 'Your people were in the theaters during the war while mine were in concentration camps! Even now, you make us stand in the street!'

"The manager became very embarrassed," Amalie says, barely suppressing a small smile. "He said the seats were filled, but that we could have the box seats, which they kept reserved for celebrities. He let us have them for free! We found out there were actually eight box seats available for us, so Norman ran outside and grabbed six people—other survivors—who had not been able to get in."

It is not hard for me to picture this scene. I can't help laughing softly.

Amalie laughs, too. "You know Norman," Amalie says, shrugging her shoulders and smiling. Then, growing more serious, she describes how they very nearly didn't make it out of Germany after all.

"All of Europe was in disarray, millions uprooted by the war," she says. "The Jews who had survived, along with everyone else in Europe, were being directed to return to their original homelands. This was ridiculous for Jews because even though the war was over, we were still in great danger. Return to what? To be killed?

"There were long lines everywhere of what they officially called 'displaced persons.' The Jews were in a particularly precarious situation because virtually none of us had a proper ID. How could we? The few of us who had survived either had assumed identities, like Norman and I, or no iden- tification at all. What kind of papers could the poor souls possibly have who were in hiding or who had been forced from their homes and sent to a death camp? So here is where there was a Catch-22. The United States was willing to let some of us immigrate, but we had to be able to prove who we were."

Norman and Amalie were frantic. "We had been through too much to be sent back to Poland," she recalls. "Finally, one day we waited outside the office of the American general consul for a man named Mr. Clark, until he returned from his lunch."

He turned out to be a sympathetic person, Amalie says with great relief in her voice. "He saw that we had been wait- ing patiently to see him, and he agreed to meet with us pri- vately. Since I spoke better English than Norman, I pleaded our case, along with all the others who spoke no English or were too sick or exhausted to fight."

"What did you say to him?" I ask, riveted.

"I told him it wasn't right that the neediest people of all, the surviving Jews, were being penalized because of bureaucracy."

"And?"

"He saw to it that the policy was changed regarding all persons who were in situations such as ours. He authorized that an affidavit from a witness testifying to a person's identity would suffice for a visa.

"I will never forget him," she adds. "He was a big, tall man, and when we left his office, he put his hands on our shoulders and wished us luck.

"'America,' he said, 'needs people like you two kids.'"

Chapter Sixteen

A ROCKY START IN AMERICA

You are lucky to be born an American," Norman tells me. "I wish I had been born an American, then I would have missed the war in Europe, the whole thing. I would be a doctor or an actor. I would have had a normal life. Tell me again, when did your parents come here?"

"Grandparents," I correct him. "In 1920. My mother's parents. My father's family have been here forever."

"Listen, it's not your fault you're half-German," Norman says suddenly. "You are a good person; it doesn't mean anything."

I'm surprised that he brings this up now. "Are you saying that not all Germans are evil?"

"Yes, I guess I am saying that," he says. "I wouldn't have believed it before, but maybe I can accept that." He seems a little amused at the idea. Then he changes the subject.

"Okay, I want to tell you about the boat ride to America," he says. "We were on a ship named the *Ernie Pyle*, an old wartime troop carrier. This was January 1947."

"How did you pay for the trip?"

"It was paid for by the Joint Distribution Committee, an organization led by American Jews that helped Jews all over the world. Under a group affidavit, we were able to immigrate to the U.S. because this organization agreed to sponsor

160

us and promised to get us jobs. My brother in America had sent an affidavit, so he said, but we never received it, so without the Joint Distribution Committee we would have been stranded."

Norman says most of the passengers were barely living Holocaust survivors. "We were all in terrible shape. And the crossing was very rough. I was so sick on the ship that I wanted to die. I was ready to give up. I remember that I prayed to God that the ship would sink!"

"And what happened?"

"Fortunately, he was not listening!" Norman chuckles at his own joke.

The men were separated from the women, he recalls. "We were packed in like—oh, what is that saying about small fish in a can? Like sardines. We were packed in like sardines.

"From upstairs, we could hear Germans in the first-class cabins. They were former officers and their families, and they had gotten proper papers to start over in the U.S. It was sickening to hear them, drinking and singing and having a party. The war was over, and we were still tormented by them. For fourteen days, the length of the trip, we had to hear this.

"Now I want to tell you something funny," he says mischievously.

"My wife was with the women, packed forty-eight to a cabin, and separated from the men. This meant I had no one to take care of me while I was sick. You know what my wife did? She sent me a message to meet her on the sea deck. She put a kerchief on my head and dressed me in a housecoat and took me to the women's section to be with her so she could take care of me!"

There was one beautiful moment on the trip, Norman tells me. "You will appreciate this because you are an American. I kept telling my wife, 'See if you can find out when we are close enough to see the Statue of Liberty.' When word got out that soon it would come into view, people put on their best clothes and struggled up to the deck. This was January 18, 1947. I will never forget the date. I put on my one good suit, which I had made to order in Munich. It was something to see, all these Holocaust survivors, half-crawling to the deck to see the Statue of Liberty. We were all so overcome at the sight of it that we wept and hugged each other."

As soon as the ship docked, however, the celebrating was over. The passengers disembarked to an enormous building. Norman and Amalie dutifully waited under the letter *S.* "This was right at dockside in Manhattan. Ellis Island was no longer being used by this time," Norman explains.

"We were so afraid that maybe our papers weren't right, and we would be sent back," Norman says grimly. "Papers, papers, papers! Your life hung on a piece of paper!"

Then a man came walking down the rows of people. He was wearing a jacket like a longshoreman working on the piers, Norman recalls. "He looked confident, like a man who knew his place. We assumed he was some kind of American official. He began calling out our name. 'Saleschutz! Saleschutz! I am looking for two people named Saleschutz!' "

The young couple were terrified, thinking they were in trouble. "Finally, my wife called out, 'We are Saleschutz. What's wrong?' Her English was pretty good, so she did the talking.

"We could not have been more surprised by what he said next: 'Welcome to America!' he cried out. 'I am Yankel, son of Raisel Rothbard.'

"Raisel Rothbard was my father's sister, and this must be, I realized, her son who was known in America as Jack. He pulled us out of the line and got an inspector to look us over immediately. All the other refugees looked at us in awe. They thought we were a big deal! Next thing we knew we were whisked through the building and out to the curb where we hopped into a waiting car. Behind the wheel was my brother Avrum [Albert, or Al]. He was twenty years older than I and had come to America a year before I was born. As the youngest of nine children, I never knew him except for his one visit back to Kolbuszowa in 1934, when I was fourteen. My father also had siblings who had come to America back in the 1880s. Again, we had very little contact with them, except for occasional letters. So I knew none of these people personally. They were strangers to me, and I didn't know what to expect."

All of these relatives of Norman's were "very assimilated, very American," he says, adding, "I'm sure that to them we seemed like we were from another planet!"

Jack Rothbard, it turned out, was not an American official. He owned a luncheonette across from the piers, Norman says, and was a very popular fellow in the neighborhood. When he heard that Norman's brother Al was going to pick them up, he decided to come along to greet them.

"Now, let me tell you about Al," Norman continues, speaking so fast I can hardly keep up. "Al was quite wealthy and lived in a house in Brooklyn. This is where my wife and I stayed the first two weeks we were in America. One of the first things I discussed with Al and the others was my name. In America, the various branches of the Saleschutz family had become Salis, Sales, Salsitz, Salashi, and even Sanders. I chose Salsitz because that is the name my brother Al used."

Then they talked about his first name. "Naftali," they told him, would never do. Norbert, Neal, and Noland were already used as variations of it in the family. Then somebody suggested Nat, but Norman rejected it because to him it sounded too much like *nyet*, which means "no" in Russian.

The name Nathan was considered, but then Norman's

brother Al said, "No, he will only get thirty-five dollars a week with that name. With Norman, now that's a fancy name, he'll get sixty-five dollars a week!"

Norman laughs aloud at the memory. "So this is how I became Norman," he says with a grin.

"By this time, I had already learned that I was what they called a *Grine Khaye* [a greenhorn animal] in Yiddish. None of my relatives seemed to know quite what to do with me."

Norman becomes more serious. "One day I went to one of my cousins to see if he could get me a job. He had a big, fancy office in Manhattan, with two hundred people working for him. I was so impressed. Sitting there, waiting to see him, I worried that my clothes looked out of fashion—the lapels were too wide—and I remember feeling awkward about my English."

"What happened?" I am almost afraid to ask.

"He did not offer me a job. Instead, he handed me a one-hundred-dollar bill and said, 'Here, take it and get off my back.' I burst out crying in front of the receptionist as I walked out. And, no, I did not accept the money. I left it on his desk. I never spoke to him again."

Norman tells me that he found out later that some of his American relatives held it against him that he had gotten married in the Old Country. "They thought it would have been better if I had come to America as a single man and married a woman here, a girl from a rich family, maybe a widow, or a divorcée," Norman says, frowning. "Then I wouldn't have had to start from scratch. Of course, I was offended by this. I thought it was insulting to my wife! I was proud of my wife. She was a beautiful, brilliant woman who spoke seven languages fluently. She was from a 'good' family, very sophisticated, educated, and cultured. And she was mine, and I loved her. And I thought they should love her, too."

This is the first time I have ever heard Norman express such feelings about Amalie, although clearly they are just beneath the surface all the time.

Norman changes the subject. "You know, in America, if you have no money, you are nobody. The funny thing is, the one uncle I had who was the poorest in the family—my uncle Shulim, a button-hole maker and a presser—was the most generous. Uncle Shulim, who was known in America as Sam Salis, had the least to offer but gave the most. He would do anything for me—or anyone for that matter."

"Maybe that's why he didn't have any money," I interject with a smile.

"Yes, yes, that's true. That's very funny. Speaking of funny, Uncle Shulim's wife, Esther, was a sister of George Burns. Another brother of my father, Max, a dentist, was married to Mamie, another sister of George Burns!"

In addition to Uncle Shulim, other relatives were especially warm and helpful, Norman recalls. "When my wife's grandmother's sister, Esther Engelstein, found out that we had not been able to have a religious wedding, she was very sad. She insisted on giving us another wedding—a proper Jewish wedding with a rabbi!—at her apartment with fifteen or twenty guests. You can imagine how good this made us feel."

Esther's husband, Isak Engelstein, was as kindhearted as his wife, Norman recalls. "He made one of the most important gestures to us, one that I will never forget," Norman says, and I swear I see a tear in the corner of his eye. "He gave me a blank, signed check and told me to fill it out with whatever amount I needed. It was close to Christmas, and he knew my customers would increase their orders. Only, he realized I might not have enough money to buy my goods. Well, I never used the check, but I always remember that it made me feel good."

In some cases, complete strangers were kind to the young couple. "One day when my wife and I were looking for an apartment in Brooklyn," Norman says, "we struck up a conversation with a man on the train. I remember how he spoke broken English with a heavy Italian accent. We had a hard time understanding each other. His name was Mr. Rosario, and it turned out he lived in the same building as my cousin Esther Rothbard and her daughter, Regina Kauf, and son Berl [called Benek]. Mr. Rosario thought very highly of my cousin and her family, who had come to America in 1938, sponsored by my uncle Shulim. They were indeed very nice people. As a matter of fact, they took us to our first baseball game, at Ebbets Field, and explained to us the rules. Regina helped me get my first job in America, at an ink factory, and her brother Berl bought me my first suit in America. He took me to a store that was called Ripley's. It was on Delancy Street in New York, and when I put on my new suit, he said, " 'Now you look like a real *Yenkee.*' He meant *Yankee!* "

"Wait—what about Mr. Rosario?"

"Oh, yes, Rosario. Because he respected my relatives, and maybe because he felt a little sorry for us, Mr. Rosario invited us to stay in his apartment rent-free! Even after he retired and returned to his family in Italy—a town in Sicily called Santanimfa—he let us keep the apartment."

Italians, in general, seemed very welcoming to the young couple, Norman recalls. "There was a big Italian market store near the apartment," he says, "and the owner came to us and offered us credit."

The young couple spent holidays with Amalie's relatives. Harold Engelstein (the son of Esther and Isak) and his wife, Dora, hosted them for many years, as did Amalie's cousins, a branch of the Petranker family, who had come to America in 1938 from Berlin.

"Leo was a young art student then and took us to see all the sights—the museums, Radio City Music Hall, the Empire State Building, the Waldorf Astoria. This was before Leo was married, and he actually brought us along on dates!"

I realize he is talking about Leo Petranker, the retired art director whom I visited in Englewood, New Jersey.

Norman smiles. "Leo helped us to have fun, to create some nice memories, to see some of the beauty that exists in the world. When we were out with Leo, we almost felt normal."

Chapter Seventeen

A CANADIAN COUSIN'S PERSPECTIVE

Well, we were shocked, just completely shocked," Marilyn Petranker Sober tells me. "I was in nursing school," she recalls, "still living at home, and a letter came in the mail one day at the end of the war. My mother opened the letter and cried out.

" 'You won't believe it!' she cried. 'Amalie is living!' "

Mrs. Sober is Leo Petranker's sister and a first cousin of Amalie's. As I visit her in the living room of her home in Toronto, Canada, she sits with her hands neatly folded in her lap, but her eyes are wide as she remembers the events of a half-century ago.

"We didn't think anyone had lived through it. The first we heard of it was from her letter. Then they arrived in the United States—Amalie with her husband, Naftali [Norman]. None of us had ever laid eyes on him before, but as far as we were concerned, he was family."

The twenty-five-year-old Amalie made a lasting impression on her younger cousin. "Oh, my goodness, she was gorgeous, the most beautiful girl, with teeth like pearls," Marilyn says. "I was only fourteen when we left Berlin for the States, and I had always heard how beautiful, how smart she was."

It would be some time—years, in fact—before Marilyn and the other Petranker relatives would learn the extent of Amalie's and Norman's experiences during the war.

"We learned more as time went on," she recalls. "Little by little, their story unfolded."

Marilyn's husband, Dr. Stanley Sober, a recently retired orthopedic surgeon, joins the conversation. The couple moved to Toronto recently after living for many years in London, Ontario, where they raised their family. Shortly after Norman and Amalie arrived in New York, Marilyn left for Palestine to volunteer her services in the war effort there. She met Dr. Sober, then a young surgeon from England and also a volunteer. When she returned to Brooklyn, he followed, and the two were married.

While Marilyn Sober recalls Amalie as being "vivacious," she describes Norman as being "almost, well, *withdrawn*" in their early years in America.

Dr. Sober, speaking with the clipped accent of his native Britain, says Norman is "a great, convivial person" who, at first, "didn't talk much about the war, the Holocaust. It was a while before we really understood the extent of what had happened."

"I think in a way we felt a little guilty," Marilyn says reflectively. "My branch of the family had been able to get to the U.S. in 1938, so we escaped the Holocaust. The only reason we got here and they didn't is because my mother's side of the family had relatives here who were able to sponsor us. And at that time you needed a sponsor to get out. We came as immigrants, not as refugees."

In addition to Marilyn and Leo, the family consisted of Leo's twin sister, Celia (now living in Florida), and their mother, Rose.

"Rose was the matriarch of the family," Dr. Sober recalls, speaking warmly of his late mother-in-law. "She took the lead on this and was very eager to help in any way she could." This was true, despite the fact that she was estranged from her husband—a brother of Amalie's father—and could just as easily have turned a cold shoulder.

"My mother always made sure they were welcome," Marilyn says. "She was just a very warm person. And my brother Leo, he took them under his wing. They were with us whenever they wanted to come on Shabbat and every holiday. In fact, they still go to Leo's or his daughter's house on most holidays.

"One more thing I remember," Marilyn Sober adds. "They had a very hard life when they got here. After they went through all that in the war, they didn't have it easy here, either. Naftali worked very, very hard. But I remember how much he wanted to indulge Amalie. He bought her a fur-collared wrap, and oh, she was so excited. It was a little bit of luxury for the first time."

Chapter Eighteen

A PAINFUL CHOICE

Luckily for the young couple, Amalie was able to find work right away, Norman is explaining to me.

"Because of her education, she was able to get a job as a Hebrew teacher at a private school," he says, "but I was having a much harder time."

What Norman was good at—being a leader, surviving in the woods, outsmarting the Germans—did not make him especially employable in New York City in 1947.

"What could I do?" he says. "My English was not so good, I didn't have education in any particular field, and I needed work right away."

In his heart, Norman says, he always thought he would end up somewhere other than the little town of Kolbuszowa, Poland, "but this was not what I expected." He was only twenty-seven years old, but he was physically and mentally worn down from the war.

"I admit I had a hard time adjusting," he says. "My first job, I got at an ink factory through Regina Kauf, the daughter of my cousin Esther Rothbard. I had lots of ideas about how to make the factory run more efficiently, but no one would listen to me. I thought it was very stupid, the way the place was run. They could have made a lot more money! Anyway, instead of listening to my suggestions, they fired

171

me. My wife, she said my problem was that in Poland I had been a big shot in the war. I had power and authority, and all of a sudden I had none."

Norman says he got very depressed, even suicidal. "I know that sounds ironic since I had fought so hard to survive the war, but it was not an uncommon reaction among Holocaust survivors. Some people killed themselves when they found out their loved ones had not survived. Others just couldn't live with the nightmares, the memories. Me? I was tired. I felt the loss of my family members very deeply. I missed them and my little town.

"Lucky for me, I had my wife. I had a reason to get up in the morning because she needed me. I understood what she had been through, and she understood what I had been through. I could look into her eyes, and she into mine, and we understood how we were feeling without saying a word. Do you know what I mean?"

I nod and smile.

"My wife, she encouraged me," he continues. "You know, I had a lot of experience as a salesman from working in my father's store so I began to look for work as a peddler. We found out there was a large Polish-speaking community in Jersey City, just across the river from New York City. So what I did was to go there by subway and train and sell my wares.

"Let me tell you about my customers. It seemed like they all were on the top floor of fourth- and fifth-floor walk-ups [apartments with no elevators]. Up and down I went, all day long, carrying my heavy suitcase! Well, I had discovered there was a need for extra-large-size underwear among the Polish housewives! These Polish ladies, they were very plump, and they could not always find their size—5X—in the stores.

"Okay, now I want to tell you a very funny story." Norman grins. He is on a roll now. He is the stand-up comic, and I am

172

the audience of one. "My suitcase broke and burst open one day on the subway. At first I panicked, thinking that the people on the subway would steal my stuff or step on it. Everyone was staring at this extra-large-size underwear that was falling out of my suitcase! You know I never miss a chance to make a joke, so I held up a pair and said, 'Anyone want to buy this? It's a seat cover.'"

The way Norman tells it, the subway car full of strangers burst out laughing, "and next thing I knew everybody was trying to help me." People picked up the underwear and helped him stuff it back into the suitcase. One man, Norman recalls, actually took off his belt and secured the suitcase with it. Norman said to him, "Aren't you going to need that?" And he said, "That's okay. I've got another one at home." Norman adds, "I guess this means he was holding up his pants for the rest of the day!"

This experience was a turning point for Norman. "God bless America, I really decided I like it here," he says, still grinning from the memory. "I couldn't believe how nice everyone was. Such generosity, such kindness. This really was a place where an immigrant could make it."

Yet soon Norman would discover that America was not free from prejudice. "The Polish ladies in Jersey City were part of a Catholic community," Norman recalls. "One day, as I reached the top floor of one of the apartments, the door was open, and I overheard a young woman say to a small child, 'If you don't behave, the Jew will come and take you away in his sack.'"

He says he just stood there in shock. When the young woman looked up and saw him, he asked, "Why did you say that?" She just shrugged and said, "I don't know. My mother used to say it to me when I was a child, and my grandmother used to say it to her when *she* was a child."

Norman tried to reason with her without success. "This is

how it happens," Norman says, a touch of despair in his voice. "It's taught to the little children. The parents, they have to stop and think about what they are saying."

Money was so tight for the young couple that they couldn't even afford their own set of dishes. "We had to be very thrifty," Norman says, smiling. "There was a movie theater in Brooklyn that was giving away one piece of dinnerware to customers per week as a promotion. That's how we got our dishes! We went to the movies once a week until we had a full set. The movies were very cheap in those days."

Despite their financial struggles, Norman says, the young couple always managed to send money to Amalie's sister Pepka and Norman's brother David in Palestine, where life was very hard and luxuries nonexistent. "We sent packages, supplies, anything they needed. It was a very high priority to us. We also, during this time, started sending money back to Poland, which was such a poor country—and still is."

After working for a while, Norman began to get his old confidence back. "One thing I decided was that I would learn how to drive a car. It was pretty clear to me that if I was going to be an American, I had to be able to drive a car."

"New York City," I interject sympathetically, "is a pretty rough place to learn how to drive."

"This is true!" Norman cries in agreement. "But I saw many people who were not very smart who had learned to drive. So I thought, *How hard can it be?*"

Norman and I share a laugh at this remark. Then he goes on: "I have to tell you a funny story about my wife. One day we were lost driving through Brooklyn. We saw a policeman, and I asked my wife to roll down her window and ask for directions. Well, as you know, my wife was brought up to be very polite. So she called to him, 'Excuse me, sir, will you be so kind and please tell me where is Myrtle Avenue?' It took her so long to say this that before she could finish, the light turned green and people were honking and I had to hit the gas! I said to my wife, 'This is America. You don't have to be so polite!'"

At another intersection, there was another policeman, Norman adds. "I rolled down my window, and I shouted, 'Hey, Mack, where the heck is Myrtle Avenue?' And the policeman pointed the way. No problem! And I turned to my wife, and I said, 'See, that's the way it's done in America.'"

Norman is laughing so hard at his own story that his face is turning red. But after the laughter dies down, he moves on to something more serious:

"My wife and I were pretty happy together. Then something happened that made us almost split up. This was 1948. We had been married three years. The War of Independence was about to happen in Palestine, and Jews the world over were hoping and praying that we would soon have a place to call our own—the State of Israel."

The problem, Norman recalls, is that he desperately wanted to go and fight. A lot of people they knew were going. For example, Amalie's cousin, Marilyn Petranker, was leaving to serve as a nurse.

"As a Holocaust survivor, I felt passionately that the Jewish people needed a refuge in this world," Norman explains. "If Israel had existed as a nation during World War II, and if the Germans had allowed Jews to leave, things would have turned out very different. But there was no place for the Jews to go."

Had there been a State of Israel, Norman adds, people such as Amalie's great-uncle Oskar Hoenigsberg (a brother of her grandmother, Rifka Genger) and his entire family would not have perished on the *Struma*, a ship loaded with desperate refugees.

Norman is referring to a terrible event that occurred in late 1941 and early 1942. In defiance of British immigration

175

restrictions, the *Struma* left Constanta, Romania, in December of 1941 bound for Palestine. The British refused to allow it to dock, even though the boat was overcrowded and no supplies were left on board. The ship remained at sea, finally docking in Istanbul. However, on February 23, 1942, Turkish police towed it back out into the open sea where it was sunk, apparently in error, by a Soviet submarine. Only one of the 769 passengers survived.

"Not even America, the land of the free, opened its arms to Jews facing certain death," Norman says somberly. "Just look at that ship, the *St. Louis*."

Norman is referring to a ship that left Hamburg, Germany, on May 13, 1939, with 936 passengers—all but 6, Jews—bound for Havana. Only 22 of the Jews were allowed to disembark in Cuba. The ship circled off the coast of the United States, within view of Miami, while authorities discussed its fate. Eventually, the ship went back to Europe, where many of the passengers perished in German hands.

"You understand why I felt I had a duty to go and serve," Norman says. "And I had experience as a military man that would be very helpful, but as the time got closer, my wife became more uneasy."

The night before it was time to leave, Norman says Amalie told him, "I have lost too many people. I can't bear to lose you, too. If you go, I won't be here waiting for you when you get back."

Early the next morning, Norman packed his things and left the apartment. "I walked to the meeting place where a bus was waiting to take us to the dock. I watched the others get on. They said to me, 'Naftali, aren't you coming with us?'"

"What did you decide to do?" I ask quietly.

"I turned and walked back to the apartment. I am still not certain if this was the right thing to do, and I feel guilty about it, but I felt a duty to my wife. She had been through enough."

176

Chapter Nineteen

Hope for a Brighter Future

W hen I was a young girl, I had thought of becoming a doctor, just like Norman had," Amalie is saying over tea and cookies. It's just the two of us again. Norman is at the synagogue for choir rehearsal.

In fact, Amalie adds, she was accepted into medical school at the Universytet Jagielonski in Cracow and attended for one semester.

"What made you change your mind?" I ask.

"I decided instead to devote myself to the relief effort, helping Jews who had survived the war but had no food, no money, no family," Amalie explains. "There was so much that needed to be done, and it couldn't wait. Also, Norman and I moved to Breslau, and there was no medical school there.

"When we got to America, my main concern was helping to put food on the table and pay the bills!" she says. "Dreams were put on the back burner."

Still, Amalie explains, she enjoyed working. "Not only did we need the money, but I liked to work. It kept my mind off of other things. Besides, I had been working for years! I was used to it, and I liked it."

Amalie starts to laugh, and I ask what is so funny.

"I must tell you about my first job in America," she says. "It was at a factory in Brooklyn where we made ties. The owner came to me and said, 'My dear lady, you don't even make the *minimum* number in a day.' He fired me after one week!"

Fortunately, thanks to her educational background, she found work as a teacher of Hebrew at private Jewish schools in New York, first, at Magen David, a school on Avenue P in Brooklyn, and later, at Etz Chaim, also in Brooklyn. "This, for me, was a better fit," Amalie says happily. "Thank God my father sent us to such a fine school and made us study!"

So all of a sudden, Amalie, who was twenty-five when they arrived in America, found herself living a life she had never imagined. "The war was over; most people were going about their lives," she recalls. "People were sick of the war and thrilled that it was over. Everyone hoped for a brighter future."

But much of the time, Norman and Amalie felt like "two lost souls," Amalie says. "We really didn't know each other very well, but we had become very attached to each other very quickly, maybe because of the war. And we had strong feelings for each other. But we were damaged people."

"Wasn't it hard to get close to another person at this time?" I ask gently.

"You might think so," Amalie replies, "but when you have lost so much, it makes you love *more*, not less."

After a thoughtful moment, Amalie adds, "Being a teacher, I think, helped save me. To be around the beautiful children every day lifted my spirits. The fact that they were Jewish children studying Hebrew was very important to me. I was keeping alive my culture. It was wonderful to see Jewish children safe and alive and just being normal children. Sometimes, though, it made me cry to look at them. I would think of all the beautiful Jewish children who had been murdered."

Amalie has a natural affinity with children. "They would

come to me with their problems. Perhaps because of my suffering during the war, I was very sensitive. I remember one little girl actually hit me once, and I took her aside. It turned out her parents were going through a divorce. She was very angry and confused. She needed comfort and attention. That's all."

The old, cruel memories would come flooding back with no warning, Amalie recalls. "There were times when I would look at the children from the window of the school building and think how innocent and happy they were, playing games in the schoolyard. Suddenly, my eyes would fill with tears. I saw in the faces of these children the face of my sister Celia and myself as a child, when the world seemed safe and happy."

It helped that Pepka, who had married and left for Palestine just as the war started, was still alive. But it had fallen on Amalie's shoulders to let Pepka know what had happened to Celia and their parents. There had been no way to communicate during the war, so as soon as the war ended and mail delivery resumed, Amalie sent a letter to Pepka and her other relatives in Palestine: three uncles (her mother's brothers) and a grandmother (her mother's mother, Rifka Genger).

Amalie suddenly smiles. "I must tell you a story that is kind of cute," she says. "Of course, I told them in the letter that I was getting married. It seems my grandma was upset at the sight of the picture I sent of myself and Norman. Because of the way Norman was dressed, Grandma assumed that he was a Gentile! After all the family had been through, it was too much for her to think that I, the only survivor from back home, had not married a Jewish boy!

"The peculiar thing is that when I wrote to her, I also helped Norman write a letter to his older brother, David,

179

who had gone to Palestine in 1933. David, in turn, was so excited when he got our letter that he decided to meet my grandma, whom we had mentioned by name in his letter.

"But when David visited her, he was surprised to find her so subdued. She poured her heart out about her disappointment, showing him the photograph. David went back to his apartment, an hour away, and returned with a different photo of Norman—this one taken with a group of boys, all dressed in traditional Hasidic clothing. Grandma was ecstatic!"

Eager to visit Pepka and the others, Norman and Amalie in 1949 boarded the first commercial flight from New York to Palestine. It was a long and tedious trip of thirty-six hours by airplane, with stops to refuel in Newfoundland, Ireland, Switzerland, and Rome.

"It was such a relief to see Pepka and the others again; it is indescribable," Amalie says. "I sat at the kitchen table and cried. I told them in detail things I had not written in my letters."

But, she adds, she was hurt by the reaction. "I was disappointed in Pepka because I felt she was not supportive enough of me," Amalie says, the hurt still evident in her voice. "I needed a lot of comforting, and I didn't get it."

"Why not, do you think?" I ask.

"On some level, I believe she just didn't want to accept what I was telling her. I think it was easier for her to act like I was having some kind of breakdown rather than hear the truth."

On the trip back to New York with Norman, Amalie recalls feeling very discouraged. "It wasn't until Pepka saw the Eichmann trial on television more than a decade later that she began to understand."

Adolf Eichmann was, of course, the German official in

charge of "the final solution" of the Jewish "problem." As such, he was responsible for the murder of millions of Jews. He disappeared after the war, but Israeli agents located him living in Argentina in 1960. He was captured and taken to Jerusalem, where he was tried and convicted of crimes against humanity, and executed two years later.

Amalie says that when Pepka saw and heard those witnesses, she realized for the first time what Amalie had been through. "That is what the Eichmann trial accomplished—at last, people everywhere learned the extent of what the Germans did! After she saw the trial on TV, Pepka wrote me a letter, apologizing.

"So, you see, being a survivor is a very complex thing," Amalie adds. "There were a lot of adjustments for everyone to make."

Amalie understands that it is difficult for the average person to grapple with the concept of the Holocaust, that six million Jews, as well as three million other "undesirables," were annihilated.

"These numbers are very hard for people to grasp," she says. "I think part of the reason that the deniers are able to say there was no Holocaust, or to claim that it was exaggerated, is that the human mind cannot comprehend it. The scale is too enormous, the atrocities too barbaric. In a way, I understand this because even my own sister did not want to believe it.

"But people had better believe it. They had better deal with it," she cries. "Because—and this is my biggest fear—unless people understand it fully, it will happen again somewhere, someday, to someone else."

Chapter Twenty

THE VIEW FROM ISRAEL

The shores of the Sea of Galilee in Israel are a long way from the cream-colored house on the corner in Springfield, New Jersey. This is, however, where one can find Mrs. Pnina Eigenfeld on a beautiful January afternoon, relaxing on a patio of a hotel in Tiberias that overlooks the fabled waters.

Mrs. Pnina Eigenfeld is Pepka, Amalie's sister.

"Darling!" she says by way of greeting, just as Amalie does. "I've been expecting you." A year older than Amalie, Pepka has a similar radiance. She apologizes for her somewhat-hesitant English, a language she does not use regularly.

The last time she saw her sister was a year before, when Amalie came to Israel for a family reunion. The two sisters speak regularly on the phone, however, and exchange letters.

Pepka, with a pleasant laugh, confirms Amalie's reminiscence that during childhood, the two were sometimes rivals, sometimes friends. "I was the oldest daughter, and the younger two [Amalie and Celia] were closer," she recalls. "My father bought me new things, like a new coat, and they got hand-me-downs. I remember her [Amalie] saying, 'Oh, Peppy, I will be glad someday when you will be married and leave!' So, you see, we took each other for granted the way sisters sometimes do."

She interrupts herself. "Do you have a sister?" she asks.

When I answer in the affirmative, she says, "Well then, you know what I mean, darling."

In time they have come to appreciate each other. "Manya," she adds, using Amalie's childhood nickname, "is the only blood relative I have left other than my children." In other words, Amalie is her sole connection to the past.

Today, Pepka is a seventy-seven-year-old great-grandmother, having created a new family dynasty of her own. Widowed for fourteen years, she lives alone in a lovely apartment in Haifa, the beautiful port city overlooking the Mediterranean Sea.

Her boyfriend, who has escorted her to the Sea of Galilee on this day, is past eighty years old and also widowed. Interestingly, he was acquainted with the Petranker family in Stanislawow before the war. When he learned that Pepka (Pnina, in Hebrew) was widowed and living near him in Israel, he didn't hesitate to ask her out. "He remembers the Petranker girls when we were really something," Pepka says with a giggle.

She does not plan on remarrying. "Oh, no, no, no. Why would I want to do that? I don't want the responsibility. I just want companionship."

Pepka, who married young and worked hard as a farm wife, clearly relishes her present freedom. She attends concerts, visits with friends, dotes on her grandchildren and great-grandchildren, all of whom live in Israel, and takes college classes. "At the moment I am studying Hebrew literature," she says proudly, "and also geography. I am learning all about that part of America you call Alaska."

Fashionably dressed in a designer pant suit, Pepka physically resembles Amalie in some ways but not in others; the smile is the same, but Pepka's eyes are blue while Amalie's are a deep, lustrous brown.

Pepka has seen Israel change in six decades from a "dusty patch of land," she says, to a modern country. "It is not always easy living here, with the political climate and all, but it is my home."

Her husband, Lonek Eigenfeld, also from Stanislawow, migrated in 1933 to what was then called Palestine. Two years later, he resettled his parents and youngest sister here, becoming members of a kibbutz called Kfar Hachoresh. (A kibbutz is a settlement community, often agricultural. It is organized under collectivist principles.) On a vacation trip back to Poland, he began dating Pepka. She was just eighteen when they married in Stanislawow on August 20, 1939—ten days, it would turn out, before the war began.

Pepka thinks of herself as a fairly passive person, and indeed, she appears less intense than Amalie. "I would never have survived the war in Poland," she says convincingly. "My sister is the strong one. She is a fighter. We have a different character. I am what you call in America *laid-back*."

Yet this is the same woman who left home at eighteen, traveling in a wagon across the Romanian border when the war started in earnest and "bombs started falling all around us." Eventually, the young couple got into and across Romania, and from there they took a boat to Palestine.

Life in Palestine was not so easy, either. To the young bride from the affluent, progressive family that enjoyed all that city life had to offer in the comparatively exciting city of Stanislawow, Palestine seemed like "a wasteland," barren not only of food and other basic necessities but also of culture.

"It was hard, hard work," she says, rolling her eyes at the memory of it. "At first we lived on a kibbutz in Nahalal. Later, we moved to a farm of our own in Kfar Baruch. If I had not been so much in love with my husband, I would never have done it."

184

She smiles and, for a moment, looks very much like Amalie. "I didn't so much like the work on the farm," she adds, "but I wanted to help my husband. My husband was a pioneer. He studied the law in Poland but gave it up. He used to say, 'I came to Israel to build the country, not sit in an office.'"

The couple raised a son and a daughter who collectively have given her five grandchildren and four great-grandchildren. Four years after her husband died, Pepka sold the farm and moved to the city of Haifa. She has the air of someone who seems satisfied with her life, proud of her contributions, content with the present. She is also, she acknowledges, very lucky that she left Poland when she did.

"We did not know what was happening back in Poland, but we knew it must be bad," she says. "They weren't letting anyone out. If they had just let them come here, to Palestine, but no! They killed them."

She recalls the moment near the end of the war when Amalie's letter arrived. "It was the first mail we received from anyone. There had been no mail service in or out of Poland for years. So our first feeling was, Manya is alive and well! Wonderful! Thank God! But then, in the rest of the letter, she wrote about the others—Mother, Father, Celia—that they were dead. I wept the whole week. I lay in bed and cried. No one could comfort me, not my husband or my child."

Accepting that her parents and sister were dead was one thing. Accepting the manner in which they died was another matter.

"Celia was just a girl. She was seventeen, a very lovely girl. If she had died for any reason, it would be a tragedy. But to be murdered like that! And my parents, too! It took a long time until I could accept that I had no parents. I was so lonely. I

185

dreamt about them. I *liked* my parents. My parents gave us a good education. They spoke nice to us. They taught us how to live, how to behave. They were very loving parents."

All over Palestine, people were getting letters similar to the one Amalie had sent. Pepka's husband received a letter from a niece, orphaned and alone. "She was only fourteen years old," Pepka recalls. "We sent money to have her brought here, and we looked after her. She became one of the best friends of my life."

Norman and Amalie, concerned that they would be detained by the British on Cyprus, migrated to the U.S. instead. "Maybe it is just as well because we were a very poor country in those days," Pepka recalls. "They had more opportunity in America."

In 1949, when the young couple came to Palestine to visit and Amalie introduced Norman to the family, Pepka says she admired Norman from the start. "He has a very big heart, a very good heart. He is a very good brother-in-law. He is a very important member of the family."

Seeing her grief-stricken sister in person for the first time since the war had ended was, for Pepka, a jolt of reality. "Looking into Amalie's eyes, I realized it was all true. Our parents, our sister Celia, were really dead. It was a very difficult moment for us. We cried from the heart."

There is a momentary pause, and then she adds wistfully, "She was mad at me after that, you know." She pauses again and adds, "I wish I had been more sensitive. She didn't think I was sensitive enough to what she had been through. I guess I was too busy with my own feelings."

The two sisters smoothed things over and remain close. "I am, of course, very, very happy that she survived," Pepka says. "I can't imagine how it would have been if she had been killed, too."

Pepka adds that Amalie and Norman were very supportive of the challenging lifestyle Pepka had chosen in Israel. "They did what they could to help, even when they couldn't really afford to," even paying for a refrigerator, a much-coveted luxury item in Israel at the time, Pepka says.

How often, these days, does she think about the Holocaust? "From time to time," she replies, "especially holidays." Four times a year, she lights a candle in synagogue, participating in a special prayer service.

"I am not one to dwell on the past," she says. "I do not care so much about what *was* than what *is*. I am much more caught up in the here and now."

Sometimes, she says candidly, she doesn't want to hear any more about the Holocaust. "For me, sometimes I have had enough!"

Norman is one of those persons whom she calls "a little obsessed." By way of example, she recalls a car trip from Orlando to Miami Beach during which, she says, he talked about the Holocaust most of the way. "I think it was five hours."

But, she is quick to concede, there is one very important difference between her experience and that of Norman or Amalie. "It is harder for them because they lived through it," she says. "I wasn't there. I was here, safe in Palestine. Frankly, I have always been amazed and impressed by what they did."

My conversation with Pepka is on my mind several days later when I visit Yad Vashem, the famed memorial to the Holocaust in Jerusalem. Yad Vashem is conducive to thinking and to analyzing one's feelings. High on a hillside overlooking Jerusalem's rocky terrain, the memorial feels halfway to God.

Trees have been planted in honor of each "righteous

person" who helped Jews during the war. Some of the people are famous; most are not. All of their stories have been certified by Israel and placed here for all the world to see and acknowledge. Here, in this triumphant garden, good wins out over evil. Here reside the spirits who were the best of humankind.

Several days later, in a stylish suburb of Tel Aviv, I am knocking at the door of the home of Naomi Hacohen, a cousin of Amalie's. She is expecting me.

Naomi's father, Philip, was a brother of Amalie's mother, Frieda Genger Petranker. (Frieda had four brothers: Max, Philip, and Josef made it to Palestine; Herman was killed along with his family in the Warsaw ghetto.)

"Amalie's and Norman's story is very different from most Holocaust stories because they managed to stay out of the camps," she says. "It shows how hard, how very hard it was to survive outside the ghetto. Sometimes I have heard young people criticize the survivors, saying, 'Why didn't more just run away and live in the city or in the woods?' Well, it wasn't that easy. And I think it is very important for people to know that."

Naomi, a musician and music teacher at the professional level whose students include some of the finest classical pianists in Israel, is the mother of three grown children and two grandchildren. Her husband is a district court judge.

Relaxed in her beautiful home, the windows open to catch a fresh January breeze, Naomi looks far younger than her fifty-eight years. She recalls Amalie and Norman's first visit to Israel in 1949, and many trips thereafter.

"They were a young couple, very handsome," she says. "She was a beautiful, charming woman with a strong will. I do remember that her meetings with the family were full of tears. She wept and wept."

At the age of eleven or twelve, curious about Norman's

and Amalie's experiences, Naomi read "all about" the Holocaust, so much so that she would dream about it at night. She reached the point, she says, where she stopped reading about it altogether for many years.

"You cannot escape it here in Israel," she says. "Everyone was affected by it."

Her own father fled Germany at age thirty, abandoning a lucrative chain of delicatessens that he had built from the ground up, because he was convinced of the severity of the Nazi threat.

"A Nazi soldier came to get a neighbor and took him away, and he pointed at my father and said, 'Maybe we should take him, too.' That was enough for my father. He took with him his mother and a few other relatives who wanted to go.

"It was not an easy thing to do, to walk away from his businesses and come here to Israel. It was a rough life here, especially then. But it was a great decision. A very great decision by a young man."

She is anxious to point out that her father *bought* certificates to go to Palestine for himself and the others. "This is why so many Jews did not come to Israel," she says adamantly. "They were too poor."

Her father met her mother in Israel. She, too, had fled the German threat in Europe. "She was from Poland; she was a Zionist," Naomi says. "She studied nursing in Vienna because she had heard they needed nurses in Palestine and she wanted to help. She was very brave to leave Poland and come to a new country."

Her mother managed to secure passage to Palestine literally by the luck of the draw. "She went to a party and won a [cash] prize, and it was exactly enough to buy a ticket to get to Palestine in 1936."

While the war began in earnest in Europe, her parents met

and married in Palestine and built a new life. She was born in 1940. Had she been born in Poland or Germany, she says, she likely would have been among those killed.

She does not think she would have the strength to live through what her cousin has endured. "Even after what she has been through, she is a woman who knows how to enjoy life," Naomi says admiringly. "For her, family is the most important thing. Because she lost her family, she appreciates the importance of it."

Chapter Twenty-one

A MIRACLE BABY

N orman very badly wanted to go fight in Palestine in 1948," Amalie says. I can see that his plan did not please her. A frown crossed her face.

"You have to understand," she tells me, "that Norman would have been a big help there, but he would have been willing to die. He felt that if Palestine had existed as a Jewish state and had been in a position to welcome Jews, his family and thousands, maybe millions of others would have survived."

Amalie stops. She takes a breath, then: "I agree with that. But I am very grateful that he did not go. I was very conflicted because I am a very strong Zionist. The creation of the State of Israel was one of the most significant events of my life because at last I felt secure. But as for Norman going to fight, I felt like I had been through enough. I was not quite twenty-six years old. How could I bear it if I lost Norman, too?"

To outsiders, she concedes, they probably looked like a normal young couple, "but we were not." The word she uses to describe them during this period is *fragile*.

One of the hardest decisions was whether to have children. "Early in our marriage, Norman and I felt we didn't want to have children," Amalie recalls candidly. "We couldn't bear the idea of bringing a child into this world! I remember thinking, *How would I protect it? Who would care for it if something happened to me?* The world hated Jews—this was plain to see."

After a few years, however, the young couple began to think differently. "Maybe we felt more secure as time went on because we were in America now. We started thinking, *Maybe it would be nice to have a baby.* It takes courage to have a child. For us it was more like—what is that saying?—a leap of faith. A *huge* leap of faith!" She smiles broadly.

"We started thinking that to have a child would continue the family line," she adds. "It seemed only natural to desire to rebuild, and the only way to do that was to start a new family of our own. Having a child, it occurred to us, would be a way to defeat Hitler."

As luck would have it, however, once they decided to have a baby, nature did not cooperate. "We went to the doctor, and there didn't seem to be anything, in those days, that they could do for a fertility problem. Such irony! Of all the people in the world to be unable to conceive! We thought it was our job to repopulate the world, and we couldn't even have one."

They considered adoption. "We were turned down because we were Holocaust survivors," she says. "This was in the 1950s. They thought we were unstable, that we could not be good parents."

This is a painful memory, a degrading one. But Amalie doesn't linger over it. With evident delight, she says, "Then, guess what! Surprise! I was pregnant. And our Essie [Esther] was born August 8, 1956. We named her Esther Celia after Norman's mother and my little sister."

Amalie was almost thirty-four years old and Norman was thirty-six, which was considered old for first-time parents in those days. "I have never been happier than when I first saw Essie. And Norman....Oh! He was so excited! So proud!

Essie was very squashed and funny-looking, and Norman and I joked that we ought to send her back, but of course we adored her."

After the euphoria, though, she felt a profound sadness. "The fact that my mother was not there devastated me," she says. "Poor one, how I missed her! I felt cheated for myself, but especially for my mother, who would have cherished this moment. And little Essie? She, too, was cheated. She would have no grandmas. I hoped in time she would forgive us."

Norman and Amalie were without the kind of support they would have had in Poland before the war. There, they would have had their mothers and fathers, aunts and uncles, sisters and so on, to offer advice and assistance. "Honestly," Amalie says with a laugh, looking back on it now, "we really did not know what we were doing! Poor Essie!"

Chapter Twenty-two

THE SUBURBAN LIFE

Amalie has gone on her daily walk on this day, two weeks after my last visit. I want to talk to Norman today about Esther, when she was born and when she was a little girl.

Norman has a special smile whenever he talks about Esther. "She was a cute little thing," he says. "I was very proud to be her father."

By the age of two or three, Esther, who was precocious, had begun to notice that something was different about her family and began to ask questions, Norman says. "We didn't want to lie to her. When she asked about her grandparents, we told her they were dead. When she asked what had happened to them, we told her they had been murdered. We didn't want to just say they had died and have her find out later. We thought it would be more of a shock and that she would feel betrayed by us.

"But my wife, she was angry at me because she felt I talked about it too much. She says I told Essie too many details, too young. Maybe she was right; I don't know. Now my daughter says the same thing about my grandson Dustin, her first child. She says I talked about it too much when he was a little fella. She asked me to stop, so I did."

During Esther's childhood, Norman was working so hard that he often got home just in time to put her to bed, he recalls. By the early 1950s he had been able to leave behind his job as a peddler of ladies' undergarments. He moved ahead to something better, but how he got started in that was purely by accident.

"*Literally* by accident!" he says with his infectious grin. "What happened was that I got into a fender-bender on the Williamsburg Bridge [in New York City] with my first car, a run-down old 1932 Chevrolet. Unfortunately, for me, I collided with a shiny new Cadillac! I thought the fella was going to kill me. We exchanged licenses and insurance information, and when he saw my name, he said, 'Salsitz? Your name is Salsitz?'

"By complete coincidence, this man knew my uncle Max, a dentist, and many of my other relatives, too. As a matter of fact, he himself was a distant relative! He told the policeman he didn't want to file a report after all, then offered to pay for my car to be repaired."

"That's a great story," I say.

"Wait! I'm not finished. I didn't get to the good part yet! This man, whose name was Max Ratner, was a sales representative for a large manufacturer of living room furniture. He decided he was going to help me. He thought I could be a successful furniture salesman on my own, but how? I had no showroom to show potential customers my wares. Well, he let me send my customers to his showroom, usually reserved for trade. And he also arranged for the factory to sell me direct.

"I worked very hard, and before long I was accumulating enough money to save for a house. My wife was able to stop working as a teacher and spend all her time with Esther. We bought a brand-new house in the suburbs of New Jersey— the same house where we live today. So you see, it was a 'lucky' accident!"

Norman loves this story so much I can see I'm in danger of him telling it all over again. "Tell me more about the neighborhood when you moved here," I suggest.

"We wanted Essie to grow up in a real American neighborhood with her own bedroom and a yard and all those things," he says. "The reason we picked this place was that all the houses were being built at the same time. My wife and I thought this was good because everyone would be new and maybe we would feel less like outsiders.

"The other thing we liked was that the other families moving in were from various backgrounds. We wanted a mix of people. That's what America is all about! We did not want to live only with Jewish people such as ourselves. On the other hand, we did not want to be the only Jews. We saw, in Poland, what can happen when people live separately. That's how suspicion and misunderstandings grow.

"Do you want to hear something funny?" Norman asks. "I will tell you. One of our new neighbors turned out to be a Catholic from Poland. And I thought, *Oh, my! We moved halfway around the world and look what we end up with right next door!* Well, they turned out to be really wonderful people. We were great friends until the woman died and the children finally moved away."

During those years, Norman continuously built up his career. "I began to invest in property, to improve it, and rent it out," he explains. "In time I became a successful real estate developer and builder. I made a good living for my family, and we enjoyed the American life. We made new friends. We belonged to a synagogue. Essie was doing great in school."

There were occasional reminders that some Americans were anti-Semitic, Norman says. "I owned property at one time in Hoboken, just a few doors down from where Frank Sinatra was born and had grown up," he recalls. "One day, when I went to my property to collect rent, my tenant got very abusive. Never mind that he was very late on the rent.

"He said, 'I wish Hitler would come back and finish all of you people off.'

"I don't know what was more shocking, his cruelty or his ignorance, because he, too, was from a minority group that Hitler detested."

There was also sometimes hostility, Norman reports, from other Jews. "One time I took my wife to the Catskills to stay at a resort hotel that was very popular with Jewish people. It was supposed to be a fun, get-away trip, but we found ourselves in a very uncomfortable situation. Americans heard our accents and came up to us and asked questions. They asked, 'How did you survive?' The way they said it, it was more like an accusation. We felt that what they meant was, 'How come you survived, and my family didn't?' It was almost as if they suspected we had done something bad in order to survive, like turn in others, which of course we had not done. At any rate, it made me mad, and it made my wife cry."

For these reasons, Norman and Amalie preferred to socialize with other survivors who, they felt, could understand them without explanation. Among them was Norman's brother Leibush, who had survived with him in Poland. He had remarried and come to America, opening a store in Brighton Beach, Brooklyn.

"Even though he was much older than me," Norman says wistfully, "there would always be a special bond between us."

Chapter Twenty-three

A NEPHEW SHOULDERS THE PAST

Beth Israel Medical Center is one of New York City's premiere hospitals and research centers, and Dr. Edwin A. Salsitz, fifty-one, is the principal investigator of a methadone research project for the treatment of opiate addiction.

Dr. Salsitz is Leibush's son.

At the end of a typically busy work day, Dr. Salsitz—or Ed, as he likes to be known—has just finished seeing his last patient. On a typical day, he would go home and walk his dog, then return to work for a few more hours. But on this day, he sets aside his usual routine.

The confident demeanor of the successful doctor dissolves as he begins to talk about the past—not his past, though it has affected him so deeply that it sometimes sounds that way.

"I wouldn't be here without Norman because my father would not have survived without him," he says. "My father was a lot older than Norman—sixteen years—and I don't think he would have made it alone. He was physically a very strong man, but that is not the only quality you needed. Norman had more wiles, more skills, the ability to manipulate a situation, to think on his feet."

There were other reasons that Leibush depended on Norman. He spoke Polish with a heavy Yiddish accent, a

198

dead giveaway to the Poles. And, according to his son, "he was probably in worse shape emotionally than Norman" because, in addition to all the other family members the brothers lost, Leibush had a wife and three children who perished at Belzec.

Ed corrects me when I use the words *died, killed, perished,* and so on. "They were murdered," he says. "I try to use that word because that is the truth of what happened."

After the war, his father met a woman who had lost her husband in the Holocaust, and they married. They had one child—Ed, or Eddie, as he is known in the family. His mother died in 2000. His father died when Eddie was seventeen.

"My parents never, ever talked about how they met," he says. "It was off-limits. They never talked about courtship, how they met. I guess they associated it with such bad times."

A good-looking man with a strong resemblance to Norman, Ed says that not having normal role models when it came to romance and marriage has affected his own life. Now divorced, he concedes that his parents' Holocaust experiences have had a negative impact on his personal relationships.

He and his former wife had no children, although, he says candidly, it was not due to a conscious decision on their part but "just the way it worked out." He is content with his work, his friends, and his dog, a rottweiler. ("As far as I know, he's not anti-Semitic," he jokes about his dog, a German breed. "I told you I've got Norman's sense of humor.")

What he is not content with, and may never be, is the Holocaust. "For me, not an hour goes by that there isn't something on my mind about it," he says. "As time goes on, it seems more and more unbelievable to me."

An avid runner who participates in the New York City Marathon, Ed says he encounters what he calls an "echo" each year when runners from Manhattan line up in midtown to be bussed en masse to the race's starting point in Staten Island. "It always reminds me of what my father said about the cattle cars, the way Jews were shipped off to the death camps," he says, shuddering. "I think of those poor souls."

He sees the universality of the Holocaust experience in modern life. "You turn on the TV; you see Rwanda or Kosovo or some other place where hatred is causing people to try to annihilate each other. And you wonder, Will people ever learn? Why don't they learn? That's all we Jews want, is for people to see what happened to us, not to feel sorry for us but because we so desperately do not want anyone to go through this again."

His father, he believes, never recovered and did not adapt to life in America as well as Norman did. "My father never wanted to be in America," he says with finality. "He wanted to be in Kolbuszowa, in his grocery store there, with his first wife and his three children. Only they were all murdered."

Leibush, who was forty-three years old when Ed was born, opened a grocery store in Brighton Beach where he talked openly and often about his murdered children, particularly the eldest, Shulim, who was twelve years old when he was gassed at Belzec. (Shulim was killed with his mother, Chancia, and two younger siblings: Shlomo, age ten, and Rosa, who was seven years old.)

"My father had a real guilt problem, I think, about Shulim," Ed says. "Shulim was already twelve, but he went with his mother and the two younger children. My interpretation is that my father may have believed that if Shulim had stayed with him and Norman, the boy might have survived."

One of Ed's most precious possessions is a letter written by

Shulim to his uncle David, Norman and Leibush's brother who survived the Holocaust because he was living in Palestine. "I used to think of the letter primarily as something of historical interest," Ed explains. "Now I am finding it harder and harder to read. It makes me cry. It's so cheerful and innocent, with this impending doom he was so totally unaware of."

For a long time, Ed did not think of these three children as his siblings. "I thought of myself—and really, still do—as an only child. I think there was a part of me, to be honest, that resented them."

Listening to him describe his childhood, I do not find it hard to understand why. "My father didn't talk *to* me about my half brothers and my half sister, but he talked *about* them in front of me to the customers," Ed says. "Sometimes, when I was working in the store as a kid, he would say I was his grandson. Other times he would say 'Yes, he is my son, but I'd have an older son if he hadn't been murdered.' He would say this to complete strangers."

Leibush also habitually talked about Kolbuszowa in glorified, idealized terms. "He would say, 'See that apple? If you think that's a nice piece of fruit, you should have seen the apples we had in Kolbuszowa!' A few years after my father died I went there. I had to see this place, this Oz, for myself. It was just a little old crummy town in Poland! Even before the war it couldn't have been as perfect as he remembered it. I felt kind of relieved and let down at the same time."

If not for his mother, Felicia Kluger Salsitz, Ed thinks the burdens of his childhood might have been insurmountable. "Fortunately, I had my mother," he says. "She was optimistic, bubbly, and liked to do things. She never talked about the Holocaust at all. As a matter of fact, I only vaguely know how she survived and what ordeals she went through."

This much he knows: his mother was in Poland during the war, hidden by a Polish Catholic. She was married with no children; her first husband did not survive, nor did her parents and a brother. (Two sisters survived.)

"Until the end, I couldn't get my mother to talk about it at all, and if I pushed too hard, she'd cry," Ed says. "Her solution was not to talk about it. It worked for her, but the irony is that I do not feel connected to my maternal family members who were murdered in the Holocaust. They were never brought to life in my memory."

He also had Norman. "I have always identified very strongly with Norman. He means a lot to me because he saved my father's life, but also because I could admire the way he was dealing with his past. He speaks at schools, he does everything he can, and I respect that."

Norman organized a family reunion of the far-flung branches of the original Saleschutz clan, helping to maintain a sense of family identity. The event, held during a weekend in 1992 at a resort hotel in the Catskill Mountains of New York State, marked a century, more or less, since the first members of the family—siblings of Norman's father—came to America. It was an eye-opening experience for everyone involved, including Ed.

"This was the first time I realized what a very diverse group of people we were. There were people from Chicago, from Israel, from you-name-it. The most interesting thing, though, was how some were so very assimilated and some were not."

(Some of them, according to Norman, did not even know they had Jewish roots. Of 145 who attended, about 35 were non-Jews. One woman was a Catholic nun.)

Norman also saved the family photographs, which has given Ed a link to his past. "I realized early in life that my father's family had faces, thanks to Norman's photographs. My mother has no photographs. None. For the longest time, when I was a kid, I thought she was hiding them from me, but the truth is, they were destroyed in the war."

Did his parents have a close marriage?

"I don't know. No. Not really." He adds, "I don't understand how these couples paired up. I just don't get it at all. There must have been tremendous need, just to have someone to hang onto."

Did he ever have a meaningful conversation with his father about the Holocaust, one on one?

"I never had a meaningful conversation with my father about anything," he answers abruptly. After a moment he adds, "That sounds terrible, doesn't it? The thing is, I loved my father; I really did. I wish he had lived longer. I understand his situation now—the things he said, the way he talked in front of me. I think it was the only thing keeping him sane.

"Do I forgive him?" he asks rhetorically. "Of course. Of course I do."

Chapter Twenty-four

LIFE AND DEATH

L eibush and I were in deep trouble," Norman is saying. "After I shot Stashek and Yashek, I was the most
wanted man in the district."

I'm anxious to hear the rest of this story, but I'm steeling
myself. Listening to Norman tell me his adventures and
tragedies is more intense than watching any Hollywood-
made suspense film.

"Naturally, the Germans had figured out what had happened," Norman says. "They finished off Stashek, and now
they knew to look for us. Remember I told you that I tried to
grab our things in the dark before we ran away, but that I
couldn't? Well, the Germans had found our things, including
my sister Rachel's diary written in Yiddish."

Meanwhile, news spread among the Poles that two of the
best AK leaders had been killed by Jews. "The AK placed a
100,000 zlotys reward on my head," Norman says, "but I did-
n't feel remorse for what I had done. Why should I? I had
acted in self-defense. I felt so betrayed. How could I ever
trust anyone again after this?"

Norman sits at his desk chair with his arms folded tightly
across his chest. "What would you have done?" Norman
asks me.

"The same thing, I suppose," I say.

Although Norman's wounds from the gunshots were healing pretty well, the condition of Leibush's feet was a deep concern. Running for miles barefoot, crashing through ice on a pond, Leibush suffered with feet so mangled that Norman silently feared his brother would never walk again or perhaps die from infection. He would need a place to recover.

"With help from our friend Lyba, I managed to get him to Franek's barn," Norman says. Franek was the local Pole who had delivered merchandise to Norman's father's store before the war and had helped him by contacting the group of Jews living in the woods.

Leibush was to stay at Franek's for two weeks while his feet healed. But one night when Norman sneaked in for a visit, Leibush told him that he suspected he was being watched. In addition, Franek had been bringing Leibush his food each day at 5:00 P.M., but that day he had not shown up yet. Eventually, he came around eight o'clock with a bowl of cold soup, Norman says. That, in itself, seemed odd, because he always brought hot soup.

"When Franek finally arrived with the soup, I stayed hidden," Norman recalls. "I no longer trusted him, based on the things Leibush was telling me. When Franek left, I told Leibush not to eat the soup. I had a bad feeling. But Leibush was hungry and took a spoonful. Immediately, he spit it out. I could see by his violent reaction and the look on his face that he had been poisoned! I ran down to the barn, quickly milked one of the cows, and brought some of the milk to Leibush. I forced him to drink the milk and then told him to stick his finger down his throat to throw it all up."

Leibush was okay, but both brothers were badly shaken. They gathered their belongings and quickly left for the only place they had a chance—the forest. Only a few members of the original group were still alive, but at least they had each other.

Norman began to worry that Monsignor Dunajecki, who

had given him the birth certificate, must feel betrayed. "I figured that he must have heard what happened to Stashek and Yashek," Norman says. "It really, really bothered me. I wanted him to hear my side of the story. It was incredibly risky, foolish even, but I went to Kolbuszowa late one night to tell him."

Monsignor Dunajecki had indeed heard about the brothers, but he thought they had been killed by the Germans and considered them to be patriotic heroes, Norman explains.

"And you told him what really happened?"

"Yes," Norman says.

This is how Norman remembers the conversation:

" 'Father,' he said, 'I have a confession to make.'

" 'Go ahead.'

" 'I killed them.'

" 'You what?'

" 'I killed them in self-defense.' " After Norman described every detail, the kindly priest reacted strongly.

" 'This is outrageous!' the monsignor replied. 'It is painful to hear these things. I am a man who loves the truth more than my very life.' "

Norman adds that without hesitation, the monsignor announced that he would write to the bishop and request that the bodies of the two brothers, who were buried in a place of honor, be reinterred by the wall, like common criminals. "As I left," Norman says, "he wanted me to take a pair of his shoes, but I refused. I kissed his hand and left. I never saw him again."

In a bizarre twist, Norman, who was still intent on fighting the Germans in one way or another, found a way to *join* the AK. It was a different subgroup, he explains, one that operated outside the area. No one knew him, and he used his false ID as a Catholic Pole, Tadeusz Jadach. That was only about two months after the deaths of Stashek and Yashek.

Norman was happy during that time. "We raided a police station in Glogow and disarmed the police. We blew up the railroad between Lvov and Cracow several times. We attacked Ukrainian villages near the San River in reprisal for the killing of some members of the AK. At last I was getting to do my part in the war effort!"

Along with his comrades, Norman was treated as a hero by the Polish people in village after village. "But I never forgot that if they knew who I really was—Naftali Saleschutz, a Jew—I would be murdered instantly," he says ironically.

His days with the AK ended when a member of his unit learned that a Jewish family was hiding in an underground bunker under a barn in a nearby village. "It was immediately decided by the leadership," he recalls with disgust, "that my comrade should go to the place where these Jews were hidden and kill them, along with the peasants who were hiding them."

Norman, thinking quickly, volunteered for the mission, too. Here is how he describes what happened:

"My comrade from the AK and I set out on our assignment. It took about two hours on foot to get there. When we arrived, he was a few paces in front of me, and I shot him. I killed him! What else could I do? Stand by and watch him kill innocent people?

"After it was over I shouted in Yiddish for the Jews to come out of hiding. It turned out to be a young man, his girlfriend, and her younger brother. I had saved their lives, but they had nowhere to go. I took them to join Leibush and the last few Jews of our original group in the forest. This would be my 'home' again, too, since I certainly had just ended my days with the Polish resistance."

"What happened to the young people you saved?"

Norman looks at me sadly. "They did not survive the war." He continues. "The forest was swarming with combat troops by this time. The Russian front was very close. It was rumored there were Russian partisan groups already in the forest with us. I wanted to meet their leader. I still hoped to fight the Germans!"

Through Stashka, Norman was able to make a contact. At the appointed day and hour, he went alone. "As soon as I reached the area where I was told they were hiding out, a voice called out to me to raise my hands over my head," Norman recalls. "I did as I was told and was marched to a clearing where about eighty men and their horses were gathered."

He explained to the leader that he was from a group of Polish partisans looking for his counterparts among the Russians. "I didn't dare risk saying anything about us being Jews," Norman says gravely. "I told them that I had a plan to wipe out some Germans at an SS substation near Pustkow, but I didn't have enough men to pull it off."

Their leader was very receptive to Norman's plan. "Over the next week," he says, "we worked together to come up with a strategy. Four times, several of us went over there at night to study the layout of the buildings and the land. This was March of 1944."

Saturday night, when the Germans routinely gathered for a party at the substation, was the target night. "There were twenty-one of us in all—fifteen Russians and six from my group of Jews," Norman recalls, his hazel eyes gleaming. "It took us more than two hours to get there by horseback. Four of us, including myself, took the lead. We wore German uniforms so as not to arouse suspicion."

I'm not sure I want to hear this part, and I sigh. Norman looks at me closely. "Should I keep going?" he asks. "Are you okay?"

"Sure," I lie.

"As we got close to the compound, we left our horses in the woods," he says. "The five of us in uniforms crawled to the barn opposite the farmhouse. The rest surrounded the house from the rear and both sides.

"The lights were on, the windows open, and I could see right into the place. The SS men were drinking and flirting with the girls. My main target, I was glad to see, was also present: the Scharführer. This man—if you can call him that—had my friend Motek beaten to death. He also had once mocked the God of Israel in my presence. These incidents happened while I was a slave laborer, and I vowed that one day, if I had the chance, I would pay him back.

"One of the Russians climbed up a telephone pole and cut the wires. Within seconds, the five of us in German uniforms crept up to the house. It was a nice night, and the windows were wide open.

"The explosions from the hand grenades we tossed through the windows rocked the ground. The sky lit up. The Germans, after a moment, began to shoot back. All around me was gunfire, but I thought, *At least if I die now, I'll go down fighting!*

"I had been given a submachine gun, a Pepesha, from the Russian commander. I felt like a lame man suddenly able to walk. With the others, I fired round after round into the house until no one shot back at us. The farmhouse was completely ablaze. We set fire to a storage facility and the car and some motorcycles. And then we left, bringing the Germans' horses with us."

We sit in silence for a while. "Gee, Norman," I say weakly. "Remind me never to get on your bad side."

He laughs, and I smile despite myself. I'm actually feeling a little sick. He killed those Germans—including women. They were, genetically speaking anyway, my people. But those particular individuals were not good people. Even the women, although not soldiers, could not possibly be called innocent bystanders, because if there is one thing I have learned from Norman and Amalie, there was no such thing as an innocent bystander.

"You did the right thing," I say finally.

Not one of the Germans present that night survived, Norman tells me. The German authorities, he adds, were mystified. "Apparently, they concluded that the attack had been led by Poles," he says. "In reprisal, they killed two hundred Poles in Pustkow."

I don't know how much more of this I can hear today. I am longing to get in my car and return to my house at the seashore and get back to my tidy little life. But Norman is determined to go on.

"I parted with the Russian group after this. I would have loved to stay with them, but as the front was moving closer, it seemed more important that we Jews stick together, on our own. Our group had once numbered 125. Now we were just six, most of us killed not by Germans but by Poles.

"Many roads in the area were jammed with retreating German soldiers, tanks, and equipment. All night long we heard cannons booming. Each day, the sounds grew closer, and our hopes grew higher!"

Norman's face is flushed with the excitement of remembering. "Liberation was so close, but I almost didn't live to see it," he says. "One night, I was with Lyba late at night when some peasants went by on horseback. Lyba thought I should go ask them where the shooting was coming from. He was certain he knew them and said that since he would be recognized by them immediately as a Jew, I had to be the one to ask.

"At first I hesitated, but Lyba had never been wrong. I ran

after them and called out, and the two men slowed down and turned. To my horror, they were SS men.

"I was dressed as a peasant, so it flashed through my mind that I should pretend I couldn't speak a word of German. So I started babbling in Polish excitedly. I said I was a farmer searching for my wife and children. One of the Germans knew some Polish and translated to the other. I was hoping they would send me on my way, but they decided to take me with them.

"One of them had his gun drawn on me while I was speaking, but as he got back on his horse, he put the gun back in the holster. This was my moment, and I had to act fast. I took out my revolver and shot them both dead. I took their guns and used the horse to shield me as I left the area, but as I reached the edge of the forest, a voice ordered me to stop. It was a Russian! I had no choice but to surrender the horse and four guns and go with *him*. I was taken to a group of Russians and made to wait for their commander. I had some explaining to do, they said."

There are tiny droplets of sweat on Norman's brow and forehead. I think, *He is an old man. I hope he doesn't have a heart attack.*

"The Russian commander arrived wearing a beautiful leather jacket and riding an impressive horse," Norman says. "He listened to my story and congratulated me for killing the two Germans. He even invited me to join his group, but I told him I had to get back to my people. As I walked away I worried they might shoot me in the back, but it didn't happen."

"What about Lyba? Where was he during all this?" I ask.

"Oh, Lyba," Norman says with a smile. "I have to say I was a little annoyed with him. I saw him again later that night, and he was really shaken up. He said he felt like killing himself because he thought I had been killed and it was his fault."

That night the two of them hid in a barn belonging to an old woman Lyba knew named Baba, Norman recalls. At five in the morning, Norman heard someone enter the barn. He peered down and was startled to see a Russian soldier. He was holding a cup in his hand, apparently hoping to get some milk for his breakfast. Norman called down, greeting him in Russian.

"He was a friendly fellow and told us how he and his comrades had just liberated Kupno and were now on their way to Kolbuszowa," Norman says. "It took a moment or two to sink in. The presence of this Russian soldier here meant only one thing—we had been liberated!"

Leibush had spent the night hiding somewhere else and had already heard the news by the time Norman found him. "We were ecstatic, but we didn't know what to do next," Norman recalls. "We still had enemies all around us. Leibush and I talked it over. I believed that for now, Jews would probably be safer in a larger town. Later that day, we set out for Rzeszow. This was at the end of July 1944."

Once again, Norman's instincts were correct. Other Jews were not so lucky. Norman describes what happened to his friends Naftali Kanner and Leibush Nessel, two Jews who went back home to Kolbuszowa as soon as it was liberated:

"They were from our original group in the forest. They had survived all this time, all the way to liberation. In Kolbuszowa, members of the AK had taken charge when the Germans retreated. Witnesses told me later that two prominent men took my friends behind the Catholic cemetery and shot them to death."

Only 4 of the 125 people in the original group in the forest had survived—Lyba and his brother Herschel, Leibush, and Norman.

The fate of Naftali Kanner and Leibush Nessel puts

Norman almost off the deep end, even now, more than fifty years later. He paces the room, obsessed and furious.

"They were killed *after the war was over!*" he shouts. "Incredibly, this was the fate that met many Jews. What is the first thing you would do if you survived in a camp or in hiding or in the forest and the war was over?"

"Go back home, I suppose," I say meekly.

"Right! You would go back home! Well, when they returned home, often their *neighbors* killed them."

More than 2,000 surviving Jews were murdered in this way between 1945 and 1947 in Poland, Norman says. He has been accumulating eyewitness accounts for years.

The most well-known of these crimes was the pogrom at Kielce on July 4, 1946, which has been studied by historians for decades. It was started by the wild tales of an eight-year-old boy, a Christian, who had run away from home for three days. When he returned, he told his parents—apparently in an attempt to avoid punishment—that he had been kidnapped and tortured by Jews. He also said he had seen several dead Christian children in the basement where he had been a captive. There was no evidence that any of the boy's allegations were true.

"The official report even noted that the house where the boy was supposedly held didn't even have a basement," Norman exclaims. "It was next to a river!"

But the local population believed a bizarre legend that Jews used the blood of Christian children to bake their matzohs (especially after the Holocaust, it was said, since survivors were "undernourished"), and the boy's story was accepted. A mob gathered, and the rest is history: forty-three Jews were murdered, and fifty were injured. Thirty more Jews were taken off trains running between nearby cities and murdered on the spot. Ironically, many of the Jews were planning to leave Poland, hoping to get to Palestine.

Before the war, there were 3.3 million Jews living in Poland. Only 50,000 survived the German extermination effort. Another 250,000 Polish Jews survived incarceration in Russian camps and made their way back to Poland after the war. "This means there were 300,000 survivors—or one-tenth of the original population of Jews in Poland," Norman says somberly. "But the Kielce pogrom, and other atrocities like it, made it clear that it was not safe for Jews to rebuild their lives in Poland."

A mass exodus began, much of it illegal. At least 100,000 Jews left Poland in the months immediately following the Kielce pogrom. "People were desperate to get out of the country, but nobody wanted us—there were strict quotas in the U.S., and the British were preventing us from going to Palestine," Norman says. The British, he adds, were anxious to please the Arab nations, due to their country's need for oil.

Norman wants to clarify something to me. Many of the 2,000 Jews who were killed in Poland after surviving the war were not, he says, killed in pogroms like the one in Kielce. "They were killed one or two at a time in isolated incidents. Sometimes the local Poles despised Jews so much that they wanted to finish off the job that the Germans had started. I have spoken to many survivors over the years where this was the case. They were greeted, upon returning from the camps, with scorn: 'You! You are back! We thought you were all dead!'"

That was not the case in all parts of Europe, as evidence shows at the Holocaust Memorial Museum and many other sources. "The Dutch and the Danish welcomed back their surviving Jews," Norman says with admiration. "In Denmark, there were many cases where Jews returned to find their homes preserved for them, with food in the cupboard and flowers on the table to welcome them back. Not so in Poland. And this is why I am so hurt, so deeply hurt and angry, at my fellow Poles."

"Was it just hatred, plain and simple?"

"No," he replies. "Sometimes there were reasons beyond anti-Semitism, such as financial gain. For instance, if someone had moved into a Jew's home and taken over his property, you can see why they would be unhappy when the true owner reappeared."

Norman has investigated the case of his two friends for years. He is still looking for additional eyewitnesses. "In the case of Leibush Nessel, I believe, one of his murderers had his own reasons to do away with him," Norman says angrily. "Back in 1939, when the war broke out in Poland, Leibush Nessel was a soldier in the Polish army, and this man was a reserve officer. Leibush Nessel had told me once that this man had asked him to get two sets of civilian clothes from the Jews in the town they were near, which was at the German border. He invited Nessel to desert with him, but Nessel refused and went on to fight the Germans. Well, this man found some other way to desert. Imagine how he felt when he saw Nessel return home after the war. By killing him, he was eliminating the possibility that his desertion, a shameful thing, might be discovered."

The Jews who made the decision to go to Rzeszow after liberation banded together in sort of a commune, Norman recalls. There the full extent of what had happened began to register. "In my hometown, there had been two thousand Jews, yet only nine remained alive at the war's end," Norman says. "I began to wonder why I had survived when others had not. Was it God's wish that I be a witness? Was it because I am a Cohen, a direct male descendant of Aaron, the high priest, brother of Moses? Was I to carry on the lineage that had been nearly destroyed?"

Norman says he couldn't sit and think about it, or he would go mad. He began to set his sights on joining the Russian Air Force. He passed all of the physical and mental exams and was accepted, but changed his mind when he was persuaded by two Polish Army officers that the war would be over by the time he was graduated two years later. The two Polish Army officers—both Jews incognito—convinced him to remain in Poland and join Army Intelligence. They also provided him with a new alias, Tadeusz Zaleski, because the AK was looking for him under the name Tadeusz Jan Jadach. He was accepted into the army, eventually reaching the rank of captain.

"I had power that, as a Jew, I could hardly imagine," he says in retrospect. "But it was a phony life since no one really knew who I was. While my Polish military comrades made plans for their futures in liberated Poland, I felt I had no real reason to live."

Indeed, no one would have recognized Naftali Saleschutz. Instead of wearing the unadorned clothing of a traditional Jew, he wore a uniform. Instead of having a flowing beard, his face was clean-shaven.

"The loneliness I felt was indescribable. I missed all my loved ones. But I missed me, too. I didn't even know who I was anymore."

"What kept you going?" I ask after he pauses a long time.

"Well, as a Polish army officer, I was able to help many Jews who remained in great danger," Norman says. "This is what kept me going."

"For example?"

"For example, one day a peasant came to me and offered to show me where a Jewish family—it was a man, his wife, and two little boys—was still hiding. He said to me, 'I can take you to them so you can finish them off. All I ask is that you give me their rags.'"

Norman explains that he hid his rage and arranged for the peasant to go for a ride, along with Yanek, a Jewish friend who was also posing as a Christian in the army. "Yanek and I questioned this man out on the frozen ice of the Vistula River," Norman says. "We got the details from him about this one Jewish family, but also the names and locations of other Jews in hiding.

"The man kept saying, 'I just want to help out. They said the Polish army was going to kill the Jews who were still alive, to clear Poland of all of the Jews.' Yanek took out his revolver and finished him off with two shots."

"And what," I'm almost afraid to ask, "happened to the Jewish family in hiding?"

Norman smiles triumphantly. "I made arrangements for them to be moved to safe places. And this I am proud of, for I was able to protect innocent men, women, and children who would otherwise not be alive."

Chapter Twenty-five

IN THE LIONS' DEN

The events in her life leading up to the day she would meet Norman were "like something out of a movie," Amalie tells me. "It just got crazier and crazier.

"I was living in Cracow, hoping to survive the war there incognito, when I began to have more problems with my ID," Amalie says tensely. "My employer at the club, Mr. Zeidel, wrote out a *Bescheinigung*, a letter of employment, with my new name. This was a help, but what I really needed was a fake birth certificate so that I could get a proper *Kennkarte*."

At that time, she still did not yet know Norman.

"Once again I turned to Mundek. I wrote to him in the hope that he could find a priest who would create such a document. Amazingly, Mundek was able to come through for me once again; it arrived in the mail shortly after. But when I applied for my card, I received a summons saying there were 'certain irregularities' in my application!"

The memory of it still makes her gasp. "What was this about? Well, it turned out that while my application stated I was Roman Catholic, the stamp at the bottom of the birth certificate indicated Greek Orthodox! Playing the role of the innocent little girl once again, I just acted like it must be a mistake."

She wrote another letter to Mundek, she says, and thankfully, a new document arrived with the correct information.

"Now all I needed was to have my picture taken," she says. "Not a big deal, right? Well, I found a photographer on Karmelicka Street who agreed to take my photo. When I returned to pick it up, though, I had one of the greatest shocks of my life."

There, in the front window of the store, on a busy street in the second-largest city in Poland, was an enlargement of Amalie's photo.

"Can you imagine the danger? It's amazing the stress didn't kill me. I went in, and I told the photographer that I was flattered but couldn't understand why he had selected my picture for the store window. 'Oh, but my dear Miss Milaszewska, this is one of the best photographs I have ever taken,' he said. I pleaded with him some more, but then stopped. If you argued too much, it could arouse suspicions.

"Then I had an idea. I told him that I am running away from my boyfriend and that the picture would endanger me! This worked, and he took the photo down."

Despite her own concerns, Amalie wanted to get involved in the underground movement. "The Warsaw ghetto uprising had made a lasting impression on me," she explains. "It inspired me to think about what I could do to help. I realized I was in a unique position, working for a German concern."

Amalie says she suspected that a girl named Yanka, one of the girls she had worked with at the club, might have a contact in the Polish underground. It was, Amalie says, "just a hunch." She approached Yanka one day and told her she was interested in working for the underground. Yanka, she adds, did not seem surprised. A week later she informed Amalie that she had spoken to her contact and that Amalie's name would be placed on their list. In this way, Amalie became a member of the Zelbet Company of the AK, whose leader was "Przemyslaw."

"Yanka gave me the telephone number of a man called 'Tadek,' with instructions to call him if I had any useful information," she recalls. "We were to maintain strict anonymity because the underground was under constant German surveillance."

Amalie was still working for the Langert Construction Company at the job that the handsome German businessman, Jurgen, had helped her obtain. It really began to appear that the war might end soon. The Allies had invaded France, and the Russians were pushing the Germans back from the Russian front.

By the summer of 1944, with the Russians approaching, the Langert Construction Company started to move back to Germany. "The last thing they wanted was to be caught by the Russians," Amalie says wryly. "I had to find a new position quickly."

Langert referred her to Herr Kern, manager of the Organisation Todt in Cracow. Organisation Todt, named after one of Hitler's chief military engineers, worked behind the lines, building fortifications for the Wehrmacht, Amalie explains.

"Herr Kern hired me as a secretary. I worked there for about two months while the entire firm also returned to Germany. Toward the end of the summer, I was able to get a recommendation for a different job, this time at a Viennese construction firm, the M & K [Meyereder & Krauss] Construction Company, which was still operating in Cracow."

Amalie describes this as "an incredibly anxious time, in some ways the worst time of the entire war." The Russian forces had advanced all the way to Rzeszow, a two-hour train ride from Cracow, but then stalled there. The end was in sight, tantalizingly close. She considered escaping to the Russian side. She tried to imagine what her parents would want her to do and decided to stay put.

Meanwhile, at work, she received a marriage proposal. "I met a handsome young Polish man named Cesiek, the son of a man who held a high government position in Lvov," she says. "We dated a few times, and he fell in love with me."

Cesiek often talked about how much he hated the Germans, Amalie recalls. "However, there was one thing he said they had done right: ridding Poland of Jews! I wasn't too surprised to hear him say this because it was a common feeling among the Poles. I was so furious. How I wished I could say to him, 'You might like to know, by the way, that I'm Jewish. Do you still want to marry me?' "

As the Russian troops continued to advance toward Cracow, the M & K Construction Company made plans to evacuate, Amalie says. Her boss asked her to go back to Vienna with him to work in the main office, but Amalie said she couldn't leave, "since Poland was my homeland."

Before he left, Amalie says with a sly smile, he called her into his office, gave her a check for two months' salary in advance, and assured her with great confidence that he would return when the Germans recaptured Cracow (which, as it turned out, never happened). He went on to say that she should expect an important phone call from the military commandant.

"And so, you see, I was left in charge of the office of a powerful German-controlled company, one directly tied to the war effort," Amalie says, smiling broadly now. "I even knew the combination of the safe. And I was waiting for a phone call from the German commander!"

It was during this thrilling and chaotic time that she would meet Norman.

Chapter Twenty-six

AN IMPOSSIBLE TASK

I think it takes a certain kind of personality to get through what they did," Esther Dezube says, perched in a chair at her dining room table. "What I mean is, I don't think it was an accident that they survived."

She and her husband, Bruce, are relaxing while the boys have settled down to do their homework. "My mother is very strong," she says, "and my father is very rebellious."

Norman would argue publicly with anyone who crossed him, she says. Amalie was less confrontational, but expressed herself in ways that were "just as intense."

"You must realize that when I stepped on a bug, my mother said, 'Like Germans killing Jews.' That was my perspective on life."

Esther has a gentleness about her, a studied patience, and candid words that might seem strong are softened by a smile. There is no sense that she is critical or angry. And it's not, as she herself points out, that she was neglected. Quite the contrary.

"I was smothered by their love," she says. "I was absolutely smothered. Even when I first started dating, you know my mother would hover around the phone, writing down things she thought I should say! This is why I had to leave home and go away, out of state, to college. I needed the distance. I told them that, too. And although they don't agree with it—they think a daughter should live nearby her parents—they have accepted it. I think."

There was absolutely no compromise, however, on the subject of marrying a Jew. "I had male friends who were not Jewish," Esther says, "and that was fine with my parents, but marrying any of them? That was not an option."

Did they specifically tell her they wouldn't accept it?

"I don't recall my parents actually saying it," she says slowly, "but they let me *know* that it would destroy them, and my feeling was that they had been through enough. I could never do that to them."

They also let her know from a very early age that it was very important to them to become grandparents one day. As an only child, she knew that this responsibility fell squarely on her shoulders, but fortunately, she says, she always wanted children. "It really wasn't an issue, thankfully," she says.

"They are wonderful grandparents, and it is good for the boys to know them," she says. "They were ecstatic when Dustin was born, and they were ecstatic all over again when Aaron and Michael came along."

From time to time, especially with Dustin, the first grandchild, Esther says she asked her father "to tone things down a little bit about the Holocaust. I had to assert myself that Bruce and I would decide when and how much the boys would hear about it.

"I was always the one who would care for injured birds," she adds. "I couldn't understand how anyone could walk past something that was suffering and needed help."

It is fairly common for children of Holocaust survivors to be unusually compassionate and to feel compelled, in a role reversal, to protect their parents. So says Dr. Sylvia Hammerman, a psychologist with expertise in treating such people and herself a child of Holocaust survivors.

"Children of survivors are under a lot of pressure," she says over breakfast at a restaurant near her private practice in Newtonville, Massachusetts. (It is coincidence that she and Esther live nearby each other in the suburbs of Boston. The two women have never met.) A petite woman with a head full of curls, Dr. Hammerman outlines the typical problems of the children of Holocaust survivors.

"There are two levels of issues, the primary one being the realities of having no relatives, of the direct consequences of the Holocaust. And secondarily, the effects on the parents who went through all that and how it plays out on the children."

Her professional interests have expanded beyond her personal experience, even encompassing children of German perpetrators who are anguished about their parents' participation in the war. She works with a group called TRT, which stands for To Reflect and Trust, in which children of survivors and children of perpetrators meet once a year, since 1992, in a group session held alternatively in Germany, Israel, or the U.S.

"The perpetrators' children have tremendous shame," she says. "They really feel they've been tainted in some way. One of the men in the group decided not to have children because he didn't want to pass on 'bad seed.' "

While most people in the group had fathers who were high-ranking Nazis, feelings of guilt and shame "are not uncommon among the entire German population," Dr. Hammerman says. "They feel they are affiliated by nationality."

The two "sides" face each other at the TRT meetings, and somehow, after much discussion, the sessions usually result in both groups feeling a new sense of peace. Or relief. Or something.

"It's not always clear what they feel, but they usually say, 'I feel better.' "

Like Esther, Dr. Hammerman is an only child. Her parents, now in their eighties, live in New Jersey and are friends of Norman and Amalie, part of the tightly knit network of Holocaust survivors.

"It took me a long time to even understand why I was different from other kids when I was growing up," she says. It wasn't until she read a magazine article about children of Holocaust survivors when she was thirty years old—a piece in *The New York Times Sunday Magazine* by the writer Helen Epstein—that "a gong went off in my head." She realized that she had "been trying to make up for all the dead people.

"And that," she adds, "is one impossible task."

Chapter Twenty-seven

"GET THE PLANS
AND KILL THE GIRL"

When my daughter was little, one day she asked me, 'How did you and Daddy meet?' Every child asks that question sooner or later," Amalie says with a smile.

"Well, I wished I could have told her that we met at a dance or at synagogue, or that we met through friends. Or that he carried my books to school or something like that.

"But that is not how it was!"

Norman was masquerading in the Polish army as an officer named Tadeusz Zaleski. Meanwhile, she was masquerading as the young Polish woman, Felicia Milaszewska.

"I want to tell you how it happened," she says simply. "Norman and his comrades arrived in Cracow, the first Polish unit to enter the city. Orders arrived from the Russians that he and his group were to handle a very dangerous problem. Throughout the city, the Germans had constructed hollow columns, each about one story high and three feet square, and filled them with enough dynamite to destroy substantial sections of the city. Important historical buildings were also wired with explosives. The Germans' plan was to blow up the historic city of Cracow as a way of slowing down the Russian troops or, if need be, to stop a Polish uprising. Altogether, 287 places were mined.

"Norman and his comrades, working with Colonel

Kostenko of the Fifty-ninth Russian Army, were to work with Russian intelligence in preventing the destruction of the city. The Russians had tried to dismantle several of these columns on the outskirts of the city, but it was slow and extremely hazardous work."

Amalie takes a deep breath. "Knowing the Germans' obsession with orderliness," she continues, "Norman was convinced that somewhere there probably existed a master plan. He learned that in the building across from the M & K Construction Company, there were eight Polish girls living in an apartment who had worked as maids for the Sonderdienst, the auxiliary SS unit recruited from citizens of Ukrainian descent. The Sonderdienst had occupied the building before the Russians attacked. Norman and his comrades paid a visit to these girls, and with the help of a little vodka, the girls provided some important information. A German girl, they said, had been left behind in the offices of M & K at 19A Juljusza Lea Street."

Three men, Amalie says, were sent to apprehend the "German girl," but they came back an hour later. They were prevented from going in by an iron gate and concrete bunker in front of the building. Norman, with his comrades Yanek and Roman, decided to go himself, Amalie says. The date was January 17, 1945.

"Their assignment? 'Get the plans and kill the girl.'

"When they got there, Yanek wanted to shoot the lock off, but Norman yelled, 'Wait!' He saw a girl peeking out of a window just above them. Suddenly, a man appeared behind the gate. He identified himself as the custodian and insisted that everyone else had left.

" 'That can't be,' Norman said. 'I saw someone at the window.' "

Amalie clears her throat and continues, "The man must

have feared them, for he went and got the key and simply unlocked the gate. They followed him to an apartment on the first floor, where they saw a woman, perhaps thirty-five years old, approaching. She was the daughter-in-law of the owner of the building. She led them into a larger room farther down the hall. It was a beautiful room: crystal chandeliers, brass wall sconces, and brass floor lamps, illuminated paintings in gilt rococo frames. Three young women stood in the corner staring at them. Two were Slavic-looking girls, who were maids.

"The other was me—the 'German' girl."

Norman, Amalie recalls wryly, immediately singled out the "German girl" as the one he was looking for. "What is your name?" he demanded.

"Felicia Milaszewska."

"This a Polish name, but aren't you a German?"

"No, I am Polish."

"Don't lie," Norman yelled. "We have information that you are German."

"You are wrong. I am Polish."

"Where were you born?"

"In Wilno."

"Isn't this the office of M & K Construction Company?"

"No, these are the living quarters for the company's personnel. The offices are across the hall."

"Who is in charge here?"

"I am—or rather I was."

"What are you talking about? How can you be in charge? Do you think I'm going to believe that such responsibility was given to a Polish woman?"

"I was told by my boss that they would all return in a few weeks, and I was ordered to manage the office until then," Amalie said. Then she added, "I thank God that the Germans seem to be losing the war. I will no longer be in their employ."

He was livid. "How well you have rehearsed your part! Ha, you are glad your people are losing the war! You're not fooling me. Why would Germans put a Pole in charge of a German concern engaged in military operations? Go ahead, you're so clever, let's hear your practiced answer."

Amalie says that she was furious at him for his manner. "You don't believe me. Here is my *Kennkarte*. Here is my most valuable possession, my identity card. See my name on it? If there is anything you would like to know, please take me to your superiors. I will explain everything."

"You will explain everything to *me*. Maybe your good looks brought you favors in your lifetime, but just this once it means nothing. I can see through you as clearly as I can see out the window. If you know what's good for you, start cooperating. My patience is short. Admit you're a German, and let's get on to other matters."

Amalie's brown eyes are more intense than I have ever seen them as she recalls these events. "He unbuttoned his coat and put his hands on his hips. This made his revolver apparent to everyone in the room. He stood there, rage on his face. Yanek, his friend, seemed somewhat less frightening. I thought Yanek might be Jewish, and I thought, *Maybe I should talk to him before the angry one [Norman] shoots me.*

" 'Please,' I said, pointing to Yanek. 'Let me talk to him in private.' Norman nodded that this would be okay, but I knew I only had a moment to try and explain things to Yanek. Yanek and I went into an adjoining room. I was right; Yanek was Jewish! Not only that, but I was able to prove to him that I, too, was Jewish, for in talking to Yanek I learned that his first cousin, Oscar Margulies, had been a classmate of mine at the Jewish gymnasium! Thank God for this coincidence.

229

Now my hope was that Yanek might be able to protect me from that other man."

Yanek and Amalie walked back into the other room. "I'm sure it seemed very odd to the others that we were laughing," she says. "Yanek took Norman aside—away from the Polish maids and daughter-in-law of the owner of the building. He whispered to him, 'This girl is not German; she's Polish. Not only that, she's a Jew!'

"Norman thought he was crazy. 'Look,' Yanek told him, 'go over and talk to her yourself. You'll see.'"

Norman came over closer to Amalie. "Tell me, did you make up your mind what nationality you are?" he asked sarcastically. A moment later he asked, "Do you speak any other language?"

She realized he wanted to hide their conversation from the others in the room, who very likely spoke only Polish and German.

"Yes," she told him, "I speak German, Russian, English, and..."

"English? Good." In broken English, he asked, "From what nation do you come?"

"I am Jewish, and I can prove it."

"How?"

"I can speak Hebrew."

"Say something."

"Why? You won't understand. It shows on your face that you have no love for Jews."

It never occurred to her, she says, that Norman might be Jewish. "A Jewish officer in the Polish army? Never! And he didn't look Jewish; he looked Slavic," she explains.

Norman was becoming more impatient. "Just say something," he demanded.

In Hebrew, not thinking he would understand, she said:

"You are a fool, and I wish you would stop questioning me."

To her surprise, he seemed to know what she had said. Yet he still didn't believe she was Jewish.

"You are very clever!" he said to her angrily. "No Jewish girl can speak Hebrew so fluently. Where would you have learned it? Obviously, the Germans got someone to teach it to you so you could mingle among Jews and spy on them."

"You are mistaken," she replied in English. "How can I convince you? What if you make a mistake and kill me? How will you live with yourself when you find out I am a Jew?"

"Okay," he said, trying to trap her. "When do Jews pray Kol Nidre?"

"On Yom Kippur, of course," Amalie replied. Then she realized: *How would he know to ask that question? Could it be that he was a Jew?* She could feel tears filling her eyes. She could hardly get the words out of her mouth. "How do *you* know about Kol Nidre? Oh, my God, can it be that you, too, are Jewish?"

Norman stood there staring. "His eyes, too, were filling with tears," Amalie says. " 'Yes,' he said. 'I am Jewish.' "

"And so this is how we met." Amalie gets up to pour coffee.

"But what happened next?" I am literally at the edge of my seat.

"Well, we just stood there grinning at each other," Amalie says. "It was the most unlikely thing either of us could ever have imagined."

"What about the others in the room?"

"Except for Yanek, they had no idea what was going on because they didn't speak the languages we used."

"But—then what?"

"Well, suddenly it occurred to Norman that here he was staring at me, but there was work to be done. He said he knew that M & K had built the dynamite-filled columns that were everywhere in Cracow, and that he was looking for a master plan, if it existed. And I said, 'Oh, why didn't you say so? I'm the one who notified the AK two days ago that I had the master plan in my possession.'"

During the next few moments, Amalie recalls, she explained to Norman how this had all come about, how her boss had returned to Austria and she was told to expect an important phone call from the commandant of the German combat forces in the Cracow area. Indeed, a few days later, when the phone rang, it was the commandant, and she had made a split-second decision.

"Oberfeldkommandantur spricht!" he announced. *"Ist das das Buro M & K Gesellschaft?"* he asked. (Is this the office of M & K Construction?)

"Jawohl," Amalie answered, trying to sound calm.

"Springen Sie die Säulen!" he instructed and hung up. (Blow up the columns!)

She could have said, "Wait a minute! The company employees have left, and your soldiers will have to blow up the columns." But she didn't. Instead, after he hung up, she picked up the phone and called her contact in the underground.

"The information was so important that I think my contact was shocked," Amalie recalls. "But obviously, he passed on the information to the correct people—who turned out to be Norman and his comrades. The only missing piece of information was that I was not, in fact, a German, and this had endangered my life."

As Amalie recounted all of this to Norman, "the expression on his face completely changed. In fact, he looked like he wanted to kiss me, not kill me." She laughs.

"To think of a Jewish girl in this situation! It is unbelievable," Norman told her. "You deserve some sort of medal."

They walked across the corridor, Amalie recalls, and she opened the wall safe. She handed him the set of blueprints. "With my compliments," Amalie said gaily.

"Thank you," he said. "This is a very important moment."

They chatted quietly, Amalie recalls. "I told him how I came to be Felicia Milaszewska and, even more strangely, how I came to be in charge of a German construction company.

"Norman replied, 'My God, what tricks life plays. It's like something out of a novel; only it's real! Thank God I didn't kill you. I'm sorry I was so hard on you.'"

It was time for Norman to go, but somehow, Amalie says, she knew she would be seeing him again. "There was a connection between us. I thought he was very handsome, and he told me later he thought I was very beautiful. But there was much more to it than that. We were two Jews who had survived in this brutal world! Somehow, in the bizarre and convoluted way that we met, it seemed like we were meant to be together."

Amalie appears lost in the past, smiling as she relives the moment.

"But what about the explosives?" I'm anxious to know. "Did the columns blow up or not?"

"The explosives were neutralized after Norman returned to headquarters with the plans," she says. "The job was done by engineers under Colonel Kostenko of the Fifty-ninth Army, Colonel Svinchenko of the Forty-second independent brigade of engineers, and Colonel Muranow of the Twenty-second brigade.

"The historic city of Cracow was not destroyed," she adds proudly. "Someday you will go see it, and you will think of Norman and I."

Without wasting any time, "Tadeusz" began to court

233

"Felicia" ferociously. "The first thing he did was send me two loaves of bread, an incredible luxury," Amalie says. "This was better than flowers or jewels, believe me. And the gifts of food kept coming. He kept sending bread and also salamis, butter, cheese, salt pork, and other items that were almost impossible to get."

"So he wooed you with food," I tease her.

"Yes, but more important to me than the gifts of food was his generosity toward others. As word got out that I had food, people came to me asking for some. Many of them were like skeletons; they were Jews coming out of hiding or returning from the death camps. Anything they needed, all I had to do was ask Norman, and he would take care of it. Still masquerading as a Christian in the Polish army, he used his power and influence to help people."

Another point in his favor was that he never forgot anyone who helped him, Amalie says. "He sent a letter to Monsignor Dunajecki, the priest who had helped him get his false ID, and asked if there was anything he needed. The priest wrote back that there were three items: candles for the church, tea (which he loved but couldn't get), and wine for the sacraments. Norman sent a case of everything. The monsignor wrote back and thanked him but said it really wasn't necessary to send enough to open a store! Norman wrote to him again a few months later, and this is how we learned that he had recently died of cancer."

Before long, the young couple decided to marry. But they had a problem: How could they have a Jewish marriage ceremony?

"As part of Jewish custom, two married couples who had never been previously married to anyone else were supposed to attend the ceremony," Amalie explains. "Well, we couldn't find any because so many Jews had been killed. Some were in hiding or, like us, living incognito. The very few Jewish couples that we knew of were not in first marriages; they were widows or widowers who had lost their spouse in the Holocaust and remarried. We felt like the last of our kind.

"So we had to settle for a civil ceremony and a small reception. Norman made all the arrangements. He even managed to get us a splendid cake! And so we were married under our phony names in Breslau by the deputy mayor, in the apartment where we would live as husband and wife. The date was October 19, 1945."

Memories of the wedding day bring back mixed feelings. "I was very happy that Norman and I had found each other in the midst of the war, and here I was a bride, a childhood dream for many girls," Amalie says softly. "But that day I wept uncontrollably. My mother, my father, and Celia were dead. Nearly all of my girlhood friends were dead. Only one person from my hometown, Cesia Lamensdorf, the younger sister of my boyfriend, Alek, was present. It really hit me, on that day, that they were all gone, that it was forever to be like this. My life was going on without them."

She chose not to wear a white dress that day. "I was still in mourning, so I wore a black woolen dress with a white shawl-style collar made of silk georgette. This seemed more appropriate; this was how I felt."

This was not the wedding day the couple would have liked, of course. "Norman and I decided that if we were still alive at the time of our fiftieth wedding anniversary—and if we were still together!—that we would have a *real* wedding on that day. We would have a big celebration. This was what we promised each other."

Chapter Twenty-eight

HEARTACHES AND REGRETS

I have one regret," Norman says suddenly. We are eating peanuts on the patio while Amalie is at a doctor's appointment. The weather is warm enough again to be outdoors. "Do you want to hear what it is?"

He eats another handful of peanuts and chews slowly. "Ouch, my teeth hurt," he says, pointing to his mouth.

"That's your regret?" I ask him in mock amazement.

"No," he says, laughing. "Say, you are starting to have a Jewish sense of humor. You are turning into a wise guy."

"Will you please get to the point? What is your regret?"

"Okay, okay. Here is my regret: I am sorry that my mother and my sisters never got to know my wife. They would have loved her. I think they would have been very close. My wife, she is a lot like my sister Rechla, very smart and educated, very direct in what she thinks and," he hesitates, "very wonderful."

I'm a little surprised. I've known Norman for nearly a year now, and he rarely says such schmaltzy things.

Later, when Amalie returns, she asks, "What did you two talk about while I was gone?"

"Norman said some very nice things about you," I say.

"Oh, shush!" Norman says.

Amalie laughs and goes into the house.

"Okay, so do you have any more regrets or any other big

236

proclamations?" I ask, getting down to business again. He doesn't say anything and appears to be mulling it over.

"I regret," he says finally, "that I can't go back in time and fix things. But some things, they cannot be fixed."

We talk about reparations—money the German government has paid out to some of the survivors. Norman accepts payment for his work as a slave laborer because, he says, "after all, I earned it." Amalie, on the other hand, refused a one-time payment she could have received for the deaths of her parents and sister. "She refused it on principle," Norman says. "She said, 'No amount of money could make up for the death of my loved ones.'"

"Is forgiveness a possibility—ever?"

"Forgiveness of the Germans? No."

"What about me? Have you accepted me?"

"I accepted you months ago."

"What if my mother's family had not been in the U.S.? What if they had been Nazis? What then? Would you have let me in the house?"

"I might still have talked to you. I think so. No, maybe not. I don't know."

"Would you go for a ride in my Audi?"

"There was a time I would not have gone near a German car, but I suppose if you were to give me a ride somewhere, I would not decline now. Maybe I am getting a little softer. But I would still never, ever buy a German car or anything made in Germany."

This is their reality. There are no quick answers, no television-style sound bites, no easy "yes" or "no." Nothing about their lives is simple.

Even within the marriage, the very relationship that has sustained them these past fifty-three years, there are issues that will probably never be resolved. On the memorial wall of photographs in the upstairs room at Norman and Amalie's house, two pictures have been added to the family collection. One is of Rozia Susskind, Norman's first love. The other is Alek Lamensdorf, Amalie's long-ago boyfriend.

"Norman feels guilty about Rozia. I don't think he has ever gotten over her," Amalie says, shrugging her shoulders wearily. Amalie insists that she was not as close to Alek. Would she have married him?

"Probably not," she says. "I mean, he was a wonderful boy, but I think I would have met many other people." Then why did she put Alek's photo on the wall?

"I didn't," she says with a defiant look in her eye. "Norman put Alek's photo there. It's his way of justifying putting Rozia's picture there." She goes on to say that she doesn't think either photo belongs alongside family members.

"Rozia, Rozia, his precious Rozia," Amalie says with sudden vehemence. "Sometimes I wish she had lived! I wish he could have married her! She remains young and perfect, a saint!"

It is true that Norman talks about Rozia frequently. While it is clear that he loved her and misses her, however, one suspects she represents something larger. It is implied, for example, when he remarks that the Germans took "everything" from him. They not only murdered his family and destroyed a way of life.

They stole the dreams of his youth.

More than a half-century has passed since the end of the war. Rozia is long dead, gassed and burned and turned to ashes at Belzec. Alek died about the same time, starved to death in the ghetto, probably buried in an anonymous mass grave. They live on, however, in the Salsitz household. Their photos hang like a question mark of what might have been.

When the talk turns to Alek, as it occasionally does,

238

Norman does not seem perturbed. There are others, however, who seem to have gotten under Norman's skin. Mention of the Hungarian count or one of the other young aristocrats who courted Amalie invariably causes Norman to comment.

"Oh, the count, the count," he will say in a mocking voice. One time, while Amalie was talking about Jurgen, the German businessman who had asked her to marry him, it was noticed that Norman left the room.

Coincidence, he says later. "I had to make a phone call." But in a more candid moment, Norman admits that when he first met Amalie, he wondered if he could measure up. "I remember thinking, *She is too good for me, too high for me*," he says. "She was a very high-class girl, very sophisticated, educated, and cultured. I was a country boy by comparison. And she was very, very beautiful. I thought maybe I would not meet her standards. But then I always tried for the best. I always tried for everything in life that was *above* what I thought I could realistically get."

Amalie overhears this from another room. She is smiling.

Seeing her there from the corner of his eye, he changes his tone of voice. "Of course," he adds loudly, "my fantastic personality and good looks made up for everything else I lacked."

"Oh, Norman," Amalie says and sighs.

Old jealousies are not the only unresolved issue in the lives of Norman and Amalie. The other is Norman's habit of calling her "Fela" (pronounced "fella"), short for Felicia, her alias during the war.

"I just absolutely detest it," she says. "I am not Fela; I am Amalie or Manya. Fela reminds me of the war! I want to put it behind me, but he won't let me! *I am not Fela!*"

Norman's defense is that he is "just being affectionate."

After all, he points out, "Fela was her name when I met her and fell in love with her."

Then there is the guilt. Norman is tortured by the feeling that somehow he should have done more to try to save his family. "Even when I go over it in my mind and I realize there was nothing more I could have done, I still feel badly," he says. "For a long time I had a sense that I had let them down." This feeling was contradicted, however, by a sense that they would be proud that he had managed to survive and bear witness.

Amalie's guilt is more focused. She feels responsible for her father's death.

"He died because he came back to look for me," she says, and her eyes fill with tears that threaten to spill down her cheeks. "He was safe, and he sacrificed himself for me. I know it is not rational, but I have always felt it was my fault."

Norman and Amalie have sought the help of other survivors, as well as a psychologist and their rabbi over the years, to try to alleviate some of these disabling thoughts. "There is only so much anyone can do to help," Amalie says. "There is a point where you just have to live with it."

Nighttime is the worst. "I have the same dreams over and over," Amalie says.

Norman, too, suffers from nightmares. "Oh, yes, all the time, every night," he says. "I do not know what a good night's sleep really is."

Are his dreams always about the war?

"Let me put it to you this way," he says wryly. "I have lived in America now for more than a half-century, and I have never had a dream that takes place here. Not once. I am always back in Poland in my dreams. Always. And it is never good."

At least, sleeping side by side all these years, they are able to curtail the nightmares and comfort each other. "Norman wakes me up as soon as he becomes aware I am having one of my dreams," Amalie says, "and I do the same for him."

The old adage that the passage of time lessens one's pain does not apply. In fact, it is the opposite. The memories and feelings have gotten more intense as they get closer to the end of their lives.

"It will be with us until the day we are buried," Amalie says.

The fact that there has been little, if any, justice only exacerbates their grief. Years after the war ended, Amalie was asked to go to Germany to serve as an eyewitness in the trials of Hans Krueger and other Gestapo men who had been stationed in Stanislawow.

"It was terrible to be in the same room with the butchers who killed my loved ones," she says, shuddering at the memory. "It was like reliving the whole experience all over again, just after we had finally moved on with our lives. But we had to do it. We just had to."

Facing the German perpetrators was so stressful for Amalie that she took tranquilizers to help her get through the experience. "We were forewarned by the Jewish Congress not to get emotional, not to cry, or our testimony would be stricken from the record," she says. "Can you imagine that? Not to get emotional?"

A few years later, she was asked to return to testify at another trial, that of the Mauer brothers who had murdered and tormented Jews in the Stanislawow ghetto while Amalie was there. It was Willy Mauer, during one *Aktion*, who had recognized Amalie and spared her life. But she had then witnessed the younger brother, Hans Mauer, shoot and kill a neighbor woman in the back.

She decided not to testify, a decision that still haunts her today. "I was physically and emotionally ruined from the first trial," she says. "It was a very difficult decision not to go, but I didn't see how I could go through that again." (The Mauer brothers were convicted anyway.)

Separate from the other trials was one in which Josef Daus was tried for "willful killing." Daus was the Gestapo man whose apartment Amalie was forced to clean as a maid in Stanislawow. (His fiancée had been friendly to Amalie when Amalie was searching for Celia.) The customary defense of the German perpetrators was to say that they were "just obeying orders" when they killed Jews. Amalie, however, had witnessed Daus kill a Jew by "pushing him against the wall and shooting him," an entirely different scenario and one that was not defensible.

Amalie testified against Daus and expected that she would be asked to attend the sentencing. In another twist of fate, she did not receive the customary plane tickets to go to the sentencing. When she inquired at the German Consulate in New York, she was told that her name was not on the list. She was advised not to go, and so she stayed home.

"It was good that I didn't go," Amalie adds, "because we found out later that the witnesses had been in danger" from an extremist group.

Many years earlier, shortly after the war's end, the Polish government had assigned Norman to assist Hewlett Johnson, the dean of Canterbury, head of an international commission that investigated German atrocities. Norman, then an army captain, was to prepare each day's itinerary and handle security. For about a month after the war, he accompanied Hewlett Johnson to most of the concentration camps in Poland, including Auschwitz, Maidanek, Treblinka—and Belzec, where his family died. Norman took his own photographs at each stop along the way, mindful that the Germans might try to downplay what had happened someday.

Only a tiny fraction of German perpetrators was ever held accountable for the acts committed during the Holocaust, a fact that makes survivors seethe. Many of the worst German perpetrators, having obtained false papers, even immigrated to the United States. In the spring of 1999, news reports detailed yet another death camp guard who had been discovered to be living all these years in the U.S. His residence was only an hour or two from Norman and Amalie's house in Springfield, a fact that had been duly noted by Norman.

"There is a part of me that would like to get into my car and drive up there and just shoot that man," he says, glowering, "but of course I won't do it."

"Why not?" I ask him.

"I don't have that right. I am a citizen of the United States, and I must abide by the laws of my country. I can't go off and kill someone."

And so Norman, who lost twenty-one immediate family members, and Amalie, who lost two hundred extended family members, are burdened with the reality that virtually all of the perpetrators will go to their graves unpunished.

The brutality of their experience has led them to question the existence of God. Ask if they are religious, and it is the only time you sense you are not getting a straight answer from Norman and Amalie. Perhaps they themselves don't really know.

They observe the Jewish holidays, but do not keep a kosher home. Norman is more involved than Amalie in the life of their temple, serving on various committees and singing in the choir. Since Norman loves to sing in front of a crowd, it is questionable how much he is participating on a spiritual level and how much he is being, as Amalie puts it rather ironically, "a ham." Norman will sing Jewish folk songs with no prompting—though "When Irish Eyes Are Smiling" is also a particular favorite.

Norman says the war certainly changed his views on God. Brought up in a religious family, he had never questioned God's existence. At this point in his life, nearly eighty years old, Norman seems undecided. "I am not so religious," he says finally.

Amalie seems equally conflicted. "I don't know what I believe," she says quietly. "I guess I would have to say that the only reason I don't say, 'There is no God,' is because I can't prove that."

Yet at times she does mention God as a real presence. When Norman wasn't feeling well recently, she mentioned that she had prayed for him. After taking him to the doctor, where all went well, she declared with certainty, "God was with us."

Chapter Twenty-nine

A POIGNANT TRIP

Has Norman ever returned to Poland? I ask the question of Amalie.

"No," she says, "and he swears he will never go back." But she adds that she went back once, in 1974, and took Esther with her. It was an important trip, Amalie says, for both mother and daughter.

"In Poland, I think she began to understand who her father had been. She learned that her mother had really lived three different lives: the happy-go-lucky girl known affectionately as Manya, the middle of three girls in a loving family in Stanislawow. Felicia, the little Polish Catholic girl who smiled during the daytime and cried all night. And Amalie Petranker Salsitz, wife, mother, grandmother, teacher, American citizen, a woman who seems accomplished and confident on the surface but who deep down cannot divorce herself from experiences in the war.

"I think that in Poland, Essie saw, with her own eyes, a place where Jewish culture had once thrived. The synagogues had been destroyed during the war or converted to a different use by the government after the war. But I was able to share with her my past, and that of her father.

"Norman refused to go. But our daughter needed this trip. You know, she is a very conscientious Jew, and I sometimes think that this trip is part of the reason."

It was in many ways a sad homecoming since there were "no relatives to visit, no great-aunts or grandmas, not even any cemeteries," Amalie says. "But Essie was able to meet some of the people who had helped her father and me during the war, who at that time were getting old but still alive."

And so they went to see the ones they could find—Amalie's "guardian angel," Mundek; the wife of her father's former Gentile boss, Mrs. Jerzenicki, who had helped her when she first came to Cracow; and Stashka (Hodur) Bardzik, who had helped Norman again and again. "They were as thrilled to meet Essie as she was to meet them," Amalie says.

"For years, until they died," she adds, "we did everything we could to stay in touch with them. Norman would send packages, food, medicine, winter coats, anything they needed. For a long time, Mundek refused any help. Finally, when he was very sick from diabetes, he accepted. We asked how much we could give him, and he said, "Would ten dollars a month be too much?" Of course, this was a very small amount of money. We sent much more than that until the day he died."

Norman and Amalie also felt that the people who had helped them should be officially recognized. "We filled out documents requesting that they be acknowledged as Righteous People by Yad Vashem in Jerusalem. Our requests were investigated and accepted as true accounts. Also, in 1987, Norman and I were able to bring the last two then surviving—Stashka Hodur and Mrs. Jerzenicki—for a wonderful visit to the U.S. They stayed in our home for three weeks. They were honored by Seton Hall University; they received keys to the town of Springfield at our city hall; they were honored by a local Catholic church. They were interviewed by officials at the Anti-Defamation League, researchers at

Yale University, and local news people. Everyone, it seemed, wanted to meet them, and they were embarrassed by the fuss. Even then, they didn't think what they had done was so special! They kept saying that it was the least they could have done, as human beings.

"When it was time to go back to Poland, Mrs. Jerzenicki said to me, 'You stayed in my house for three weeks. Now I've stayed in your house for three weeks. Now we are even!'

"I told her, 'Oh, no, we can never be even! I could never make up to you what you did for me.'"

Amalie says she was glad that Esther had a chance to know these people, who are no longer living, except for Stashka, who is ill. "I know it helped Esther to see that there were some good people in the world," Amalie says. "I hoped it would make up for the fact she had been exposed to all these stories of killings. I am her mother; I want her to be happy. She was stunted like a child born to parents who are deaf or blind.

"The strange thing is, Essie didn't give us any trouble. When she was growing up, a lot of the children were doing drugs and things like that, but Essie was a good daughter.

"I don't know how to judge myself as a mother, except to say that I think my daughter is a wonderful person, so I must have done pretty well despite everything. But I must say this about Norman: Essie could not have asked for a better father. He has always been extremely generous to her! He is totally devoted to her."

It was a disappointment, Amalie says, when Esther chose to live in the Boston area, five to six hours away by car. "She went to Boston University for her undergraduate degree, then to law school at the New England School of Law. She established her own law practice in Boston, and her husband, Bruce, is a doctor at Harvard. So she has built her entire life around Boston.

"But this is what she wanted: to build a life of her own. She made it clear. She was sweet about it, but she said she needed some distance from us.

"When she left to go to college, I don't think there were ever two parents who missed a child so much. She says she was smothered by love. It's painful, but I can see her point of view. It can't be easy to have us as parents."

Once Esther left home, Norman and Amalie were alone for the first time since Esther was born. It left more time for them to do things they had always enjoyed, such as attending the theater. "For many years there was not a Broadway show or performance at the Metropolitan Opera that we didn't see," Amalie says with excitement. Even now, they still go occasionally to see plays in the city and also at Paper Mill Playhouse, an acclaimed regional theater in Millburn, New Jersey.

And they traveled. They have lost track of the number of times they have been to Israel. But their destinations have also included South America, China, Australia, and New Zealand. Once Esther left home, they felt free to see the world, a shared ambition.

It is extremely important to Norman and Amalie that Esther is happily married, that she married a Jewish man, and that they have three grandsons to carry on the family lineage.

"When Esther was a little girl, I prayed that she would someday marry a Jewish boy. 'Oh, God, please let him be Jewish, whoever he is.'

"I think you can understand why."

Chapter Thirty

THE THIRD GENERATION: "AMERICAN KIDS"

One of the reasons I have three children is that I want roots," Esther says in her customary candid way. In this regard, she is much like her mother. She gets right to the point.

"Last year I had thirty-two people for Passover," Esther says with a big smile that reminds me more of her father than her mother. "I love to have a large group during the holidays. It makes me feel close to my faith. It makes me feel safe."

The Dezube family belongs to a conservative synagogue and observes Jewish customs. All three of the boys attend a Jewish school, the Solomon Schechter Day School, "so that they know who they are, and are proud of who they are," their mother explains.

Still, the boys are not kept isolated. They are encouraged to have friends from different backgrounds. "Their father and I stress that they are to be accepting of others," Esther says emphatically. "They are American kids, and they understand the value of diversity. I want people to accept them, and that means they need to accept others, too."

Esther points out that when she was a child in the 1950s and 1960s, to be different was to be an outsider. "Today we celebrate the differences between us," she says. "There is an emphasis on that. People are more open. I think it's better now."

249

Perhaps no one could have a greater appreciation of the social principles of tolerance and acceptance than a child of Holocaust survivors. "I have seen firsthand, through my parents, what happens when a minority group is not treated with respect," she says. "I know what can happen."

For Esther, these are simple truths. For her, the challenge in life has not been about accepting others, but to find it within herself to accept her own parents and their past, which she has inherited as surely as her mother's expressive eyes and her father's appreciation of a good joke.

"I think I'm really getting there," she says. "I think I'm becoming more understanding of what they went through. It was too much for me when I was younger, but you know this is one of the great things about getting older. You really do become more accepting."

She is even getting to the point, she says, where she can forgive them of some of the habits that, "for years, drove me crazy. For instance," she explains, "whenever we have a holiday meal here, they are late. Why? Because my father refuses to take a toll road, even though it's more direct. He'd rather sit in traffic than pay the toll! So, because of a dime or a quarter or whatever it is, we all sit here waiting for them."

She used to get mad; now she shrugs it off. "That's just the way they are. I'm never going to change them. When you think about what they went through, I think they're entitled to be a little difficult.

"As a matter of fact," she adds, "I'm really very proud of them."

Chapter Thirty-one

A LOVE OF LIFE

It's a cold and rainy day in New York City, and Norman, to Amalie's chagrin, is standing outdoors without a coat. It is an important day, the annual April observance of Yom Hashoah, or Holocaust Remembrance Day, and Norman is waiting for Amalie's arrival at Congregation Emanu-El in New York City.

"Norman, where is your coat?" Amalie yells out the window as we pull up beside him at the curb where he has motioned for us to pull over. He either doesn't hear her or acts as if he doesn't.

Striding over to a city ambulance, Norman waves his hands and can be seen speaking to the driver and his assistant. The ambulance driver, who wears a defeated look, moves his vehicle, and Norman motions us to take the space.

Amalie laughs. "Look! This is Norman! He has arranged for the very best parking place for us!"

Norman has been here since the wee hours of the morning. He is the volunteer security chief of the event, a position he has held for many years, and serves as liaison to the New York City police, fire, and emergency medical services departments.

Since speakers at the event will include Mayor Rudolph Giuliani, Governor George Pataki, and Senator Charles Schumer, serving as security liaison is a huge responsibility.

Of course, there is always the threat of terrorism to contend with. The area is swarming with FBI agents, state police, New York City police, and so on. And they all seem to know and like Norman.

"Hey, Norman, how are you?" calls out a plainclothes detective as Norman walks by.

To say that the service is an emotional one is an understatement. I have never attended such a service. As the rabbis lead prayers, hundreds of people begin to dab their eyes. By the time Cantor Moshe Schulhof sings "El Mole Rachamim," several dozen have fled the cavernous sanctuary and can be seen, sobbing, leaning against walls, doorways, and each other.

Norman and his nephew, Ed, stare fixedly at the speakers, some of whom give their presentations in Yiddish. Amalie sniffles, rummages in her purse for a Kleenex, and tries to stifle her weeping.

A strange sensation comes over me, and I realize that I feel faint. To my embarrassment, in the midst of a communal prayer, I have to push past Norman, Amalie, my husband, and Ed Salsitz and rush to an exit.

Amalie and my husband, Blair, come looking for me. Amalie is crying. "Oh, I am so sorry I invited you here. It is too much for you," she apologizes.

The people are leaving now. Like Norman and Amalie, nearly all of them are old and fragile. It is not hard to imagine that with each new year, more seats will be empty. Will the politicians still come? Will the press still cover the event?

Will anyone care?

And what about the new genocide that is occurring in the world, including in Rwanda, and in the Balkans?

These days, it is quite common for Norman and Amalie to get a phone call saying that another friend, another

Holocaust survivor, has died. When a Holocaust survivor dies as an old man or woman—as a free citizen, a human being with dignity intact—it is no small thing. It is a victory.

But then there is one less person to speak out.

I have learned much from Norman and Amalie. I have learned that no matter how bad life can be, it is possible to find—or create—great moments. They have made an art of this, culminating in their fiftieth anniversary. Fulfilling a promise they made to each other in Poland in 1945, their fiftieth wedding anniversary was the festive wedding-day party they never had.

From Argentina, from Israel, from all parts of the U.S., friends and family came to share with them on that day in 1995. It was part-wedding, part-anniversary, part-seventy-fifth birthday party for Norman, and part fiftieth anniversary of liberation from German tyranny. Only one of the 120 guests, Cesia Lamensdorf—the sister of Alek, Amalie's long-ago boyfriend—had been present at the original 1945 ceremony.

"We were not about to let that day pass without celebrating everything," Amalie explains to me, smiling. "Because, remember, darling, when you have come so close to death, when you have suffered greatly, you love life even more."

Acknowledgments

W e wish to thank the extended Petranker and Salsitz families, who accepted the intrusion into their lives with patience, good grace and humor. Throughout the project, they were candid, helpful, and self-sacrificing. In addition to Esther Salsitz Dezube and her husband, Dr. Bruce Dezube, they include Dr. Edwin A. Salsitz, Mrs. Pnina (Pepka) Eigenfeld, Mr. Leo Petranker, Mrs. Marilyn Sober, Mrs. Naomi Hacohen, and Norman and Amalie's grandsons: Dustin, Aaron, and Michael Dezube.

We also wish to thank the Reverend Blair A. Hearth, a teacher and an ordained United Methodist minister who is Amy Hill Hearth's husband of fifteen years. He has shared this journey with us.

We are extremely grateful to the staff of Abingdon Press.

Some of the personal stories here have been addressed in part in other books by Norman and Amalie Salsitz. A testimonial called *Against All Odds: A Tale of Two Survivors* was published by Holocaust Library (New York) in 1990. *A Jewish Boyhood in Poland: Remembering Kolbuszowa*, was written by Norman Salsitz (as told to Richard Skolnik) and published by Syracuse University Press in 1992. Another book by Norman Salsitz, written with Stanley Kaish, is called *Vignettes: A Harvest of Jewish Memories*, and is expected to be published soon, also by Syracuse University Press. Norman Salsitz was also a contributor to *Kolbuszowa Memorial Book*, published by United Kolbuszowa in New York in 1971. More than one hundred photographs in the latter book are from Norman Salsitz's pre-war collection.

A special thank-you is owed to Abraham H. Foxman, national director of the Anti-Defamation League, for his gifts of time, insight, and context.

Others who provided assistance include Dr. Sylvia Hammerman, the psychologist; and Naomi and Gerald Yablonsky, longtime neighbors of Norman and Amalie Salsitz.

We also wish to thank the volunteers and staff of the United States Holocaust Memorial Museum in Washington, D.C., for the use of the archives by Ms. Hearth (October 1998). Particularly helpful to Ms. Hearth were Theresa Pollin of the research department and Lauren E. Apter, a photo archivist.

We owe a similar debt of gratitude to the volunteers and staff of Yad Vashem, the Holocaust Martyrs' and Heroes' Remembrance Authority in Jerusalem, which Ms. Hearth visited in January 1999. Specifically, we would like to thank Dr. Mordecai Paldiel, director of the Department of "The Righteous Among the Nations" at Yad Vashem, for making her feel welcome.

Ms. Hearth would also like to thank Yaacov Semyatich, a Polish-born guide she hired in Israel, as well as countless others who helped make the trip a success.

Research on war criminals (Spring 2001) includes the following sources: Peter Black, senior historian, United States Holocaust Memorial Museum, Washington, D.C.; James Kelling and Amy Schmidt of the National Archives, College Park, Maryland; The German Information Center, New York City; the District Court of Muenster, Germany; and the Commission for the Investigation of Crimes Against the

Polish Nation, Institute of National Remembrance, Warsaw, Poland.

Others who should be mentioned for their support, advice, and encouragement include the Reverend George McClain, a United Methodist minister and a leading social activist in New York; John R. Firestone, Ms. Hearth's attorney and the son of a survivor; and the writer Harry Henderson of Croton-on-Hudson, New York.

Ms. Hearth is also grateful to Daniel A. Strone of Trident Media Group in New York. (And a special thank-you also to his assistant, Brenda Urban, and his former assistants, Chantal McLaughlin and Susan Boehm.)

Ms. Hearth also would like to thank Norman R. Brokaw, chairman of the board of the William Morris Agency, Beverly Hills, California, for volunteering his assistance on this project and for providing his special brand of enthusiasm and encouragement.